Word 2007 Macros & VBA

Made EASY

Word 2007 Macros & VBA

Made EASY

Guy Hart-Davis

McGraw
Hill

New York Chicago San Francisco Lisbon
London Madrid Mexico City Milan New Delhi
San Juan Seoul Singapore Sydney Toronto

The McGraw·Hill *Companies*

Cataloging-in-Publication Data is on file with the Library of Congress

McGraw-Hill books are available at special quantity discounts to use as premiums and sales promotions, or for use in corporate training programs. To contact a special sales representative, please visit the Contact Us page at www.mhprofessional.com.

Word 2007 Macros & VBA Made Easy

1 2 3 4 5 6 7 8 9 0   DOC DOC   0 1 9

ISBN   978-0-07-161479-5
MHID   0-07-161479-6

Sponsoring Editor	**Acquisitions Coordinator**	**Indexer**	**Illustration**
Roger Stewart	Carly Stapleton	Claire Splan	International Typesetting
Editorial Supervisor	**Technical Editor**	**Production Supervisor**	and Composition
Janet Walden	Greg Kettell	Jean Bodeaux	**Art Director, Cover**
Project Manager	**Copy Editor**	**Composition**	Jeff Weeks
Vipra Fauzdar,	Bill McManus	International Typesetting	**Cover Designer**
International Typesetting	**Proofreader**	and Composition	Jeff Weeks
and Composition	Madhu Prasher		

This book is dedicated to Rhonda and Teddy.

About the Author

Guy Hart-Davis is the author of more than 50 computer books on subjects as varied as Microsoft Office, Windows Vista, Mac OS X, Visual Basic for Applications, and the iPod and iPhone. His most recent books include *How to Do Everything with Microsoft Office Word 2007* and *How to Do Everything with Microsoft Office Excel 2007*.

About the Technical Editor

Greg Kettell is a professional software engineer with a diverse career that has covered everything from game programming to enterprise business applications. He has written and contributed to several books about software applications, web design, and programming. Greg, his wife Jennifer, and their two children currently reside in upstate New York.

Contents at a Glance

Acknowledgments

My thanks go to the following people for making this book happen:

- Roger Stewart, for getting the book approved and then lurking in the background, pulling strings and issuing proclamations

- Carly Stapleton, for handling the administration and finances

- Greg Kettell, for performing the technical review and providing helpful suggestions and encouragement

- Vipra Fauzdar, for coordinating the project

- Bill McManus, for editing the text with care and a light touch

- International Typesetting and Composition, for laying out the pages

- Madhu Prasher, for proofreading the book

- Claire Splan, for creating the index

Introduction

If you use Microsoft Word for work, you likely want to take full advantage of its features and get your work done as fast and efficiently as possible.

The key to getting your Word work done in the shortest possible time is to harness the power of Visual Basic for Applications (VBA), the programming language built right into Word and the other Microsoft Office applications. VBA lets you automate pretty much any action you can take interactively.

Who Is This Book For?

This book is designed to help you get started creating powerful, time-saving macros in Microsoft Word. Even if you have no experience with macros or VBA, you'll quickly get up to speed. By the end of the book, you'll be automating not only your own work but your colleagues' work as well.

What Does This Book Cover?

This book launches you straight into automating your work by using the Microsoft Office Macro Recorder, and then shows you how to build swiftly on what you've recorded. You'll learn to create macros in easy, hands-on steps rather than by plodding through theory; but you will pick up all the essential concepts of VBA programming together with the practical skills.

Here's a breakdown of what this book covers:

- Chapter 1 shows you how to start automating actions by recording macros.

- Chapter 2 teaches you how to open a recorded macro in the Visual Basic Editor so that you can examine and edit it.

■ Chapter 3 shows you how to add message boxes that let the user control the macro and how to use input boxes to get input from the user.

■ Chapter 4 walks you through creating custom dialog boxes and building them into your macros.

■ Chapter 5 teaches you how to add power to your macros by using loops to repeat actions.

■ Chapter 6 shows you how to make decisions in your macros, making your macros more flexible and adaptable.

■ Chapter 7 explains how to use variables and constants to store information in your macros.

■ Chapter 8 demonstrates how to navigate through Word's "object model" hierarchy to find the VBA objects you need in your macros.

■ Chapter 9 shows you tricks and techniques for entering, deleting, and formatting text in documents.

■ Chapter 10 covers how to create and use bookmarks, and shows you how to make the most of Word's secret, built-in bookmarks.

■ Chapter 11 explains how to create and format tables via VBA—and how to convert them to text when necessary.

■ Chapter 12 teaches you how to create and save documents and templates—and how to create and delete folders.

■ Chapter 13 covers how to remove the bugs from your macros and handle errors that may occur in them.

MEMO

Word 2007 runs on Windows Vista and Windows XP. The illustrations in this book show how Word looks with Windows Vista's Vista Basic user interface. If you're using the Vista Aero user interface, or if you're using Windows XP, your windows will look somewhat different, but everything should function the same.

■ Chapter 14 shows you how to commandeer Word's built-in dialog boxes and use them for your own purposes in your macros.

■ Chapter 15 explains how to share your macros with others and how to configure Word's security features.

Conventions Used in This Book

To make its meaning clear and concise, this book uses a number of conventions, four of which are worth mentioning here:

■ The pipe character or vertical bar denotes choosing an item from the Ribbon. For example, "choose Developer | Code | Visual Basic" means that you should click the Developer tab on the Ribbon (displaying the tab's contents), go to the Code group, and then click the Visual Basic button.

■ Memo paragraphs highlight information that's worth extra attention.

■ The Easy Way boxes show you how to get results quickly and effectively.

■ Sidebars provide extra information on important topics.

Automate Actions by Recording Macros

Want to get your work done more quickly in Word 2007? Then open the Macro Recorder and record a macro. This chapter shows you how to record a macro, how to play it back and test it, and how to create a Ribbon button for running a macro. You'll also learn how to move your recorded macro to another code module and how to delete macros you no longer need.

But first, let's make sure you're clear on what macros *are* and what you can do with them.

Understand What Macros Are and What They're For

A *macro* in Word is a sequence of commands, either recorded (by using the built-in Macro Recorder) or written down in the Visual Basic Editor, and saved so that you can run it quickly. For example, you could record a macro to format certain parts of a document in a specific way.

UNDERSTANDING VISUAL BASIC FOR APPLICATIONS

In Word, macros are recorded or written in VBA, a programming language developed by Microsoft. VBA is implemented in all the other major Office applications (Excel, PowerPoint, Outlook, and Access) as well, and it has become such a standard that many third-party companies have added it to their applications.

By using VBA, you can make one application access another application; so you can create, for example, a macro in Word that accesses Excel, Visio, AutoCAD, WordPerfect, or another VBA-enabled application.

MEMO

Code is the generic term for the program lines and program objects, such as custom dialog boxes, that you create with a programming language.

2

To do this, you switch on the Macro Recorder, perform the series of formatting actions, and then turn off the Macro Recorder.

After you record the macro, you can play it back (or *run* it) when you need to perform the same actions again. You can run your Word macro manually to format a document, or you can call the macro from another macro—for example, to perform the formatting as part of a series of tasks.

Display the Developer Tab on the Ribbon

Word provides a few macro controls in the Macros group on the View tab of the Ribbon, but the full set of controls appears on the Developer tab. Word keeps this tab hidden unless you choose to display it.

To display the Developer tab on the Ribbon, follow these steps:

1. Click the Microsoft Office button, and then click Word Options. Word displays the Word Options dialog box.

2. In the Popular category, go to the Top Options For Working With Word area, and then select the Show Developer Tab In The Ribbon check box.

3. Click the OK button. Word displays the Developer tab on the Ribbon (see Figure 1-1). The Code group (on the left) contains the buttons for working with macros and VBA.

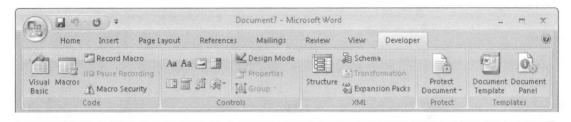

Figure 1-1   Display the Developer tab on the Ribbon to get quick access to the macro-related controls in the Code group.

Record a Macro Using the Macro Recorder

The easiest way to create a macro in Word is to use Office's built-in Macro Recorder tool. In this section, you'll record a macro that performs the following actions:

1. Opens an existing document.

2. Selects a particular section of the document.

3. Copies that part of the document.

4. Creates a new document.

5. Inserts the copied material into the new document.

6. Saves and closes the new document.

Prepare to Record the Macro

Before recording a macro, you'll usually need to prepare a bit:

- Jot down the main points of what the macro will do. Planning the macro's sequence of actions will help you avoid making mistakes that you'll then have to edit out of the macro for it to work properly.

- Launch or activate Word, and then set it up for the actions you're about to perform. For example, if you're recording a macro that will format a particular type of document, open a document of that type. As creating a macro may involve the possibility of damaging or destroying the document's contents, it's best to use a copy of a document rather than a document you actually care about.

For the sample macro, I've done the planning for you. All you need to do is take the following steps to get ready:

1. Open Word (if it's not open already).

2. Press CTRL-N to create a new blank document.

3. Press CTRL-ALT-1 to format the first paragraph with the Heading 1 style.

4. Type the heading—**Latest Report**—and press ENTER.

5. Make sure the next paragraph is formatted with the Normal style. (You should get this automatically after you press ENTER from the Heading 1 paragraph.) If not, apply the style from the Home tab's Styles box.

6. On the next line, type **=rand(4,2)** and press ENTER. Word automatically enters four paragraphs of canned text, each of which consists of two sentences.

7. Press CTRL-S to display the Save As dialog box.

8. Create a new folder named **WMME** (for Word Macros Made Easy) in your Documents folder (on Windows Vista) or your My Documents folder (Windows XP), and then save the document under the name **Latest Report.docx**.

9. Close the document.

10. Use the Open dialog box to open a document of your own from a folder other than the WMME folder, and then close that document. (This step is necessary to cause the Macro Recorder to record a change of directory when you record the macro.)

MEMO

If Windows is set to hide file extensions, you will not see the .dotm file extension.

You're now ready to start recording the macro.

Record the Macro

Follow these steps to record the example macro:

1. Click the Developer tab of the Ribbon, go to the Code group, and then click the Record Macro button. Word displays the Record Macro dialog box, shown in Figure 1-2 with settings chosen.

MEMO

The Button button and the Keyboard button in the Assign Macro To area of the Record Macro dialog box let you create a button or keyboard shortcut that runs the macro. This is handy—but if you move the macro to a different code module, as you will do in this chapter, the button or keyboard shortcut stops working. For this reason, it's best to create the button or keyboard shortcut after moving the macro.

Figure 1-2   In the Record Macro dialog box, give the macro a name and description.

5

2. In the Macro Name text box, type the name of the macro: **WMME_ Transfer_Data**.

3. In the Store Macro In drop-down list, make sure All Documents (Normal.dotm) is chosen. This is the default choice.

4. In the Description text box, type the description for the macro: **Opens Latest Report.docx, copies data from it, and closes it. Creates a new document, pastes the copied data into it, and saves and closes the document.** That may seem wordy, but it's best to make clear what a macro does so that you can easily identify it afterward.

THE EASY WAY

If you need to pause recording so that you can issue a command that you don't want to record, choose Developer | Code | Pause Recording. Choose Developer | Code | Resume Recorder when you're ready to start recording again.

MEMO

Use the Open dialog box to open the Latest Report.docx document—don't open it by clicking the document's listing on the Recent Documents list on the Microsoft Office button menu. If you use the Recent Documents list, the Macro Recorder records the instruction to open the document in that position on the Recent Documents list, not Latest Report .docx by name.

5. Click the OK button. Word closes the Record Macro dialog box and displays a blue Stop Recording button toward the left end of the status bar.

6. Click the Microsoft Office button, and then click Open to display the Open dialog box.

7. Select the Latest Report.docx document in the WMME folder, and then click the Open button to open it.

8. Press CTRL-DOWN ARROW to move the insertion point to the beginning of the second paragraph.

9. Press CTRL-SHIFT-DOWN ARROW to select that paragraph.

10. Press CTRL-C to copy the selected paragraph.

11. Press CTRL-W to close the window containing the Latest Report.docx document (and thus close the document).

12. Press CTRL-N to create a new "blank" document based on the Normal template.

13. Press CTRL-ALT-1 to format the first paragraph with the Heading 1 style.

14. Type in the words **Report Summary** and then press ENTER.

15. Press CTRL-V to paste in the text you copied.

16. Press CTRL-S to display the Save As dialog box.

17. Save the file under the name **Report Summary.docx** in the WMME folder in your Documents folder (Windows Vista) or My Documents folder (Windows XP).

18. Press CTRL-W to close the window containing the Report Summary.docx document (and so close the document).

19. Click the Stop Recording button on the status bar to stop recording the macro.

HOW TO NAME YOUR MACROS

When you open the Record Macro dialog box, the Macro Recorder enters a default name (such as Macro1) in the Macro Name box. You can accept this default name, but it's a much better idea to type a descriptive name of your own.

Follow these rules:

- Macro names must start with a letter, after which they can be any combination of letters, numbers, and underscores.

- Macro names cannot contain spaces, symbols, or punctuation marks.

- The maximum length for a macro name is 80 characters.

- Shorter names tend to be more practical, because you can see them in full in the Macro dialog box.

This book starts each macro name with WMME (Word Macros Made Easy) so that you can easily distinguish the book's macros from your own code.

MEMO

You can also stop recording a macro by choosing Developer | Code | Stop Recording—but clicking the status bar button is usually much easier.

THE EASY WAY

You can move quickly to a macro in the Macro Name list box by typing the first few letters of its name. If several macros start with the same letters, you need to type enough letters to uniquely identify the macro you want to run.

Play Back the Recorded Macro

Your next step is to play back the recorded macro and make sure it performs the actions you want. Follow these steps:

1. Open a Windows Explorer window to the WMME folder and delete the Report Summary.docx document:

   - **Windows Vista**   Choose Start | Documents, double-click the WMME folder, click the Report Summary.docx document, press DELETE, and then click the Yes button.

   - **Windows XP**   Choose Start | My Documents, double-click the WMME folder, click the Report Summary.docx document, press DELETE, and then click the Yes button.

2. Click the Word button on the taskbar to activate the Word window.

3. Press ALT-F8 or choose Developer | Code | Macros to display the Macros dialog box (see Figure 1-3).

4. In the Macro Name list box, select the WMME_Transfer_Data macro.

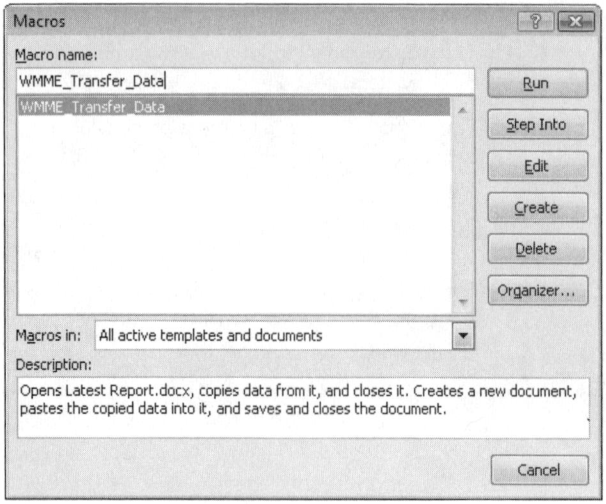

5. Click the Run button. You'll see Word open the Latest Report.docx document, select the text, close the document, create a new document, type and paste in the text, and then save and close the document—all in a second or two.

6. Return to the Windows Explorer window and verify that the Report Summary.docx document has been created again. Then close the window.

Figure 1-3   You use the Macros dialog box to run a macro you've recorded or to open a macro for editing in the Visual Basic Editor.

CHOOSING WHERE TO STORE YOUR MACROS

You stored the sample macro in the Normal template (Normal.dotm). Normal is Word's central storage location for macros, and macros in it are available whenever Word is running. The only problem is that if you create hundreds of macros, Normal may grow large enough to slow Word down.

Instead of Normal, you can store your macros in a macro-enabled document or macro-enabled template by choosing it in the Store Macro In drop-down list in the Record Macro dialog box:

- **Document**   Macros stored in a document are available only when that document is open. Use this option when creating a macro-enabled document you will distribute to your colleagues. The document must be in the Word Macro-Enabled Document (.docm) format or the Word 97–2003 Document (.doc) format, not the Word Document (.docx) format, which cannot contain macros.

- **Template**   The macro is available only when a document based on that template is open or the template itself is open. Use this option when you want to make the macro available to an entire class of document via the template the documents share. The template must be in the Word Macro-Enabled Template (.dotm) format or the Word 97–2003 Template (.dot) format, not the Word Template (.dotx) format, which cannot contain macros.

Move the Macro to a Different Code Module

The Macro Recorder stores every macro in a module named NewMacros in the document or template you specified—in this case, the Normal template. A *module* is simply a container for VBA code and can contain one or more macros. Putting all macros in NewMacros works fine if you create only a few macros, but if you create many, it's better to put different macros in different modules.

What you'll do now is move the macro you recorded from the NewMacros module to another module. Follow these steps:

1. In Word, choose Developer | Code | Macros, or press ALT-F8. Word displays the Macros dialog box.

2. Click the Edit button. Word displays the Visual Basic Editor (see Figure 1-4), opens the NewMacros module in the Code window (the main area of the Visual Basic Editor window), and puts the insertion point in the macro.

3. Select all the code of the macro from the opening Sub line to the End Sub line.

    ■ You can use the normal selection techniques that you use in Word.

    ■ For example, drag with the mouse to the left of the lines, or click before the Sub statement, hold down SHIFT, and then click after the End Sub statement.

4. Cut the macro to the Clipboard by using a Cut command. For example, press CTRL-X or choose Edit | Cut.

5. In the Project Explorer window that appears in the upper-left corner of the Visual Basic Editor window, right-click the Normal item and choose Insert | Module from the context menu. The Visual Basic Editor inserts a new code module named Module1 and displays the Code window for the module.

Project Explorer   Properties window   Code window

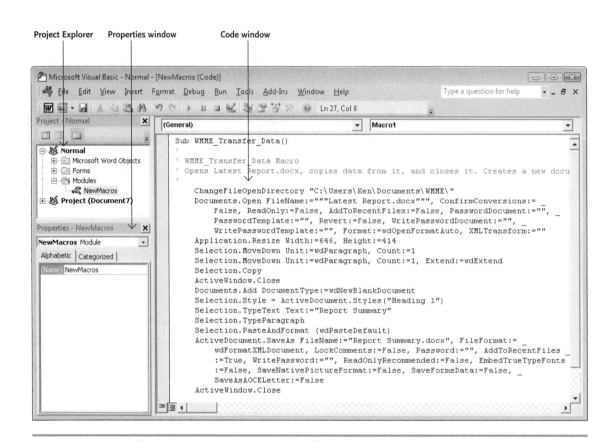

```
Sub WMME_Transfer_Data()

' WMME_Transfer_Data Macro
' Opens Latest Report.docx, copies data from it, and closes it. Creates a new docu

    ChangeFileOpenDirectory "C:\Users\Ken\Documents\WMME\"
    Documents.Open FileName:="""Latest Report.docx""", ConfirmConversions:= _
        False, ReadOnly:=False, AddToRecentFiles:=False, PasswordDocument:="", _
        PasswordTemplate:="", Revert:=False, WritePasswordDocument:="", _
        WritePasswordTemplate:="", Format:=wdOpenFormatAuto, XMLTransform:=""
    Application.Resize Width:=646, Height:=414
    Selection.MoveDown Unit:=wdParagraph, Count:=1
    Selection.MoveDown Unit:=wdParagraph, Count:=1, Extend:=wdExtend
    Selection.Copy
    ActiveWindow.Close
    Documents.Add DocumentType:=wdNewBlankDocument
    Selection.Style = ActiveDocument.Styles("Heading 1")
    Selection.TypeText Text:="Report Summary"
    Selection.TypeParagraph
    Selection.PasteAndFormat (wdPasteDefault)
    ActiveDocument.SaveAs FileName:="Report Summary.docx", FileFormat:= _
        wdFormatXMLDocument, LockComments:=False, Password:="", AddToRecentFiles _
        :=True, WritePassword:="", ReadOnlyRecommended:=False, EmbedTrueTypeFonts _
        :=False, SaveNativePictureFormat:=False, SaveFormsData:=False, _
        SaveAsAOCELetter:=False
    ActiveWindow.Close
```

Figure 1-4   You can use the Visual Basic Editor to move a macro from one module to another.

6. Right-click in the Code window and choose Paste from the context menu. The Visual Basic Editor pastes the macro you cut from the NewMacros module.

7. Press ENTER to start a new line, and then press CTRL-V to paste the macro again. (This is to give you a surplus macro that you can delete later in this chapter.)

8. Drag through WMME_Transfer_Data in the Sub line of the second macro, and then type **TestMacro** over it to change the name.

9. Press F4 to move the focus to the Properties window. The Visual Basic Editor automatically selects the (Name) property (which appears in parentheses like that), because this is the only property a code module has.

10. Type the new name, **WMME_Chapter_1**, and then press ENTER to apply it.

11. Click the Save button on the toolbar to save the changes you've made.

12. Choose File | Close And Return To Microsoft Word to close the Visual Basic Editor and display the Word window again.

Create a Button or Keyboard Shortcut to Run the Macro

Now that you've moved the macro to the module in which it will remain, you can create a way of running it. Word 2007 lets you create a Quick Access Toolbar button, a keyboard shortcut, or both.

To create a Quick Access Toolbar button or a keyboard shortcut that runs the macro, first click the Customize Quick Access Toolbar button (the drop-down button at the right end of the Quick Access Toolbar), and then choose More Commands from the drop-down menu. Word displays the Customize category in the Word Options dialog box.

You can then follow the instructions in the next section (to create a Quick Access Toolbar button) or the section after that (to create a keyboard shortcut).

Create a Quick Access Toolbar Button

To create a Quick Access Toolbar button, follow these steps from the Customize category of the Word Options dialog box:

1. In the Customize Quick Access Toolbar drop-down list, make sure For All Documents (Default) is selected. This means you're customizing the Normal template.

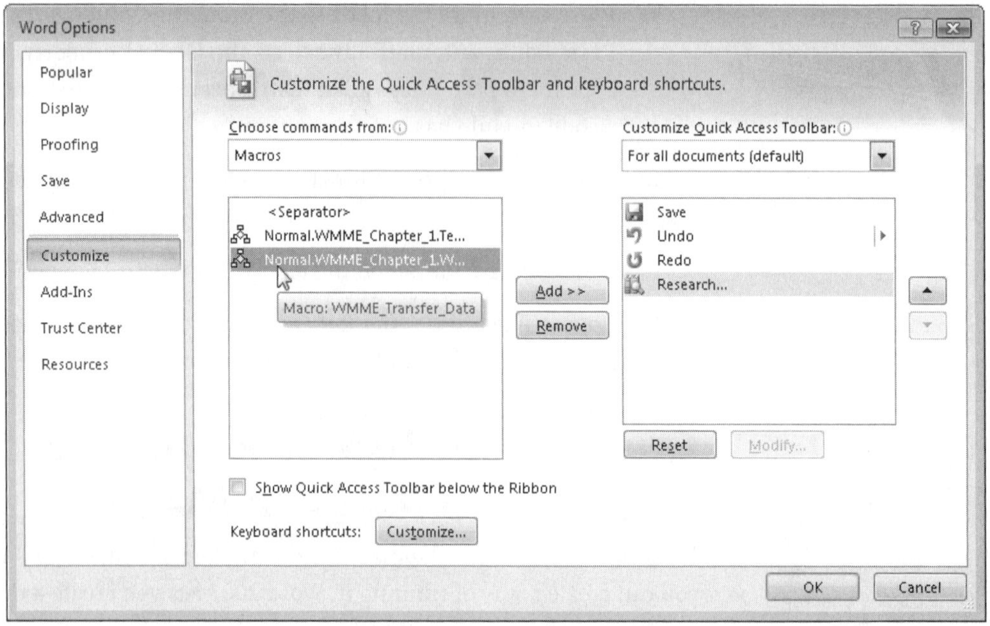

Figure 1-5   Use the Customize category of the Word Options dialog box to add a macro button to the Quick Access Toolbar. If you can't see enough of the name, hover the mouse pointer over it to display a ScreenTip.

MEMO

Word lists the macros by template or project, by module (a container for code), and name. For example, the Normal. WMME_ Chapter_1.WMME_ Transfer_Data item is the macro named WMME_Transfer_ Data in the WMME_ Chapter_1 module in the Normal template.

2. In the Choose Commands From drop-down list, choose Macros. Word displays the list of macros in the left list box (see Figure 1-5).

3. Click the Normal.WMME_Chapter_1.WMME_Transfer_Data item in the left list box.

4. Click the Add button to add a button for the macro to the right list box. The button appears at the bottom of the list.

5. If you want to move the macro to a different position on the Quick Access Toolbar, click the Up button.

6. With the macro still selected in the right list box, click the Modify button. Word displays the Modify Button dialog box, shown here with choices made:

7. In the Symbol list box, select the symbol you want to use for the button.

8. In the Display Name text box, edit the macro's name to something short and easy to understand. You're allowed to use spaces in the name.

9. Click the OK button. Word closes the Modify Button dialog box and returns you to the Word Options dialog box.

10. Click the Close button to close the Word Options dialog box. The button appears on the Quick Access Toolbar:

Create a Keyboard Shortcut to Run a Macro

To create a keyboard shortcut that runs a macro, follow these steps from the Customize category of the Word Options dialog box:

1. Click the Customize button. Word displays the Customize Keyboard dialog box.

2. In the Categories list box, scroll down to the bottom of the list and select the Macros item. The list of macros appears in the right list box, as shown in Figure 1-6.

3. Make sure Normal.dotm is selected in the Save Changes In drop-down list so that Word stores the keyboard shortcut in the Normal template.

4. In the Macros list box, select the WMME_Transfer_Data macro. Word displays any existing keyboard shortcut for the macro in the Current Keys list box.

MEMO

As with the Quick Access Toolbar, you can save the keyboard shortcut in the active document or the template attached to it instead of in the Normal template. Simply select the document or the template in the Save Changes In drop-down list.

13

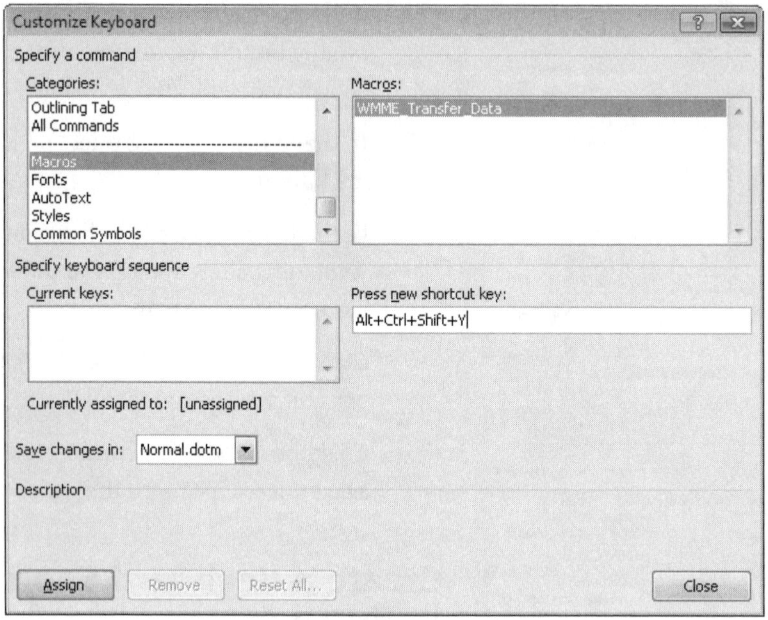

Figure 1-6 Use the Customize Keyboard dialog box to assign a keyboard shortcut to run a macro. Look at the Save Changes In drop-down list to verify that you're working in the right document or template.

MEMO

You can create a shortcut using CTRL, CTRL-ALT, CTRL-ALT-SHIFT, or ALT-SHIFT.

MEMO

To remove an existing shortcut, select it, and then press the Remove button. To reset all keyboard shortcuts, click the Reset All button.

5. Click in the Press New Shortcut Key text box, and then press the keyboard shortcut you want: CTRL-ALT-SHIFT-T.

6. Look at the Currently Assigned To readout to make sure it says [unassigned] (including the brackets). If the name of a macro or a command appears instead, decide whether you want to overwrite the keyboard shortcut. (Often, you will want to overwrite an existing keyboard shortcut, but you should always be aware that you're going to overwrite one.)

7. Click the Assign button. Word assigns the keyboard shortcut.

8. Click the Close button. Word closes the Customize Keyboard dialog box.

9. Click the Close button to close the Word Options dialog box.

THE EASY WAY

If you find you no longer need a macro's button on the Quick Access Toolbar, right-click the button and choose Remove From Quick Access Toolbar from the context menu.

Test Your Quick Access Toolbar Button or Keyboard Shortcut

Test your Quick Access Toolbar button by clicking it, or test the keyboard shortcut by pressing it.

The WMME_Transfer_Data macro runs, opens the document, copies the data, and so on, as before.

Delete a Macro

When you no longer need a macro, delete it. Follow these steps to delete the surplus macro you created:

1. Choose View | Macros | Macros | View Macros, or press ALT-F8. Word displays the Macro dialog box.

2. Select the macro in the Macro Name list box. If necessary, use the Macros In drop-down list to select the location that contains the macro.

3. Click the Delete button. Word closes the Macro dialog box and displays a confirmation message box:

4. Click the Yes button. Word deletes the macro.

Exit Word and Save Changes

In this chapter, you've made changes to the Normal template, but you haven't saved any of the changes yet.

15

MAKE WORD PROMPT YOU TO SAVE CHANGES

To make Word prompt you to save changes to Normal.dotm, follow these steps:

1. Click the Microsoft Office button, and then click Word Options to open the Word Options dialog box.

2. In the left panel, click the Advanced category, then scroll down to the Save options.

3. Select the Prompt Before Saving Normal Template check box.

4. Click the OK button to close the Word Options dialog box.

When you exit Word, the program either automatically saves changes to Normal.dotm or prompts you to save changes, as shown here. Click the Yes button to save your changes.

Edit Your Recorded Macro

In this chapter, you'll open the recorded macro in the Visual Basic Editor, examine your code, and start changing it to give it more power. I'll show you how to navigate the Visual Basic Editor's interface and how to set it up so that you can work quickly and easily.

Open a Macro for Editing in the Visual Basic Editor

First, open the macro for editing in the Visual Basic Editor:

1. Open Word as usual.

2. In Word, click the Developer tab of the Ribbon, go to the Code group, and then click the Macros button. Word displays the Macros dialog box (see Figure 2-1).

3. Click the WMME_Transfer_Data macro.

4. Click the Edit button. Word launches the Visual Basic Editor and displays the macro's code in it.

Figure 2-1   The easiest way to open a macro for editing in the Visual Basic Editor is to select the macro in the Macros dialog box and then click the Edit button.

Explore the Visual Basic Editor

Figure 2-2 shows the Visual Basic Editor with the recorded macro open. We'll now explore the Visual Basic Editor and look at its components in action.

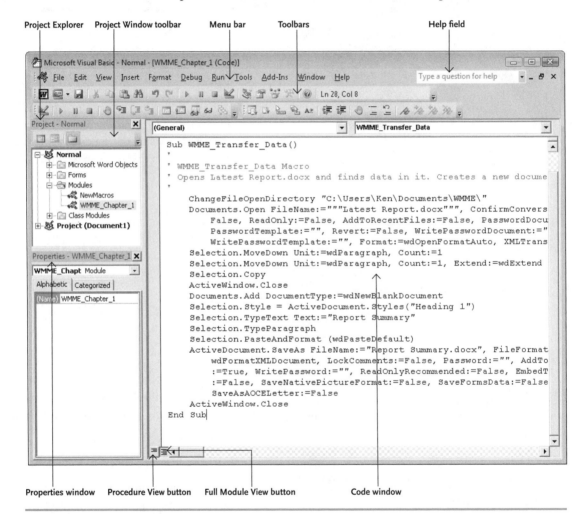

Figure 2-2   The Visual Basic Editor consists of three main areas: the Project Explorer, the Properties window, and the Code window—plus menus and toolbars.

Understand the Project Explorer

Let's start by looking at the Project Explorer window (see Figure 2-3). This is the tool you use for getting to the code items you want—macros, user forms (custom dialog boxes), and classes (custom code objects you create).

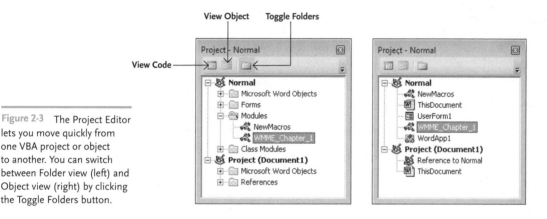

View Object   **Toggle Folders**

View Code

Figure 2-3   The Project Editor lets you move quickly from one VBA project or object to another. You can switch between Folder view (left) and Object view (right) by clicking the Toggle Folders button.

Each open document or template has its own project in Project Explorer. In Figure 2-3 you see two projects:

- **Normal**   The Normal template remains loaded all the time you're using Word, so this project always appears.

- **Project (Document1)**   This is a standard Word document that hasn't yet been saved. (Once you've saved a document, the Project Explorer shows its name.) This document is based on the Normal template; if it were based on another template, the template would appear as a third project.

You can expand the items in a project by clicking the + sign, and collapse expanded items by clicking the – sign. Once you've expanded a project, you see several folders under it:

- **Microsoft Word Objects**   This folder contains the project's Word components. Each document or template contains at least one object,

MEMO

Any template attached to an open document appears in the Project Explorer. If you've loaded another global template (for example, the Building Blocks template of canned document parts), that template appears in the Project Explorer too.

19

MEMO

Word documents in the .docx format and Word templates in the .dotx format cannot contain VBA code. If you want to put VBA code in a document or template, you must use either the Word Macro-Enabled Document (.docm) format or the Word 97–2003 Document (.doc) format for a document or the Word Macro-Enabled Template (.dotm) format or the Word 97–2003 Template (.dot) format for a template. The Normal template is a Word Macro-Enabled Template (Normal.dotm).

ThisDocument, which you can use to run code on the document or template.

- **Forms** This folder contains any user forms (custom dialog boxes) you've saved in the document or template. You'll start working with forms in Chapter 4.
- **Modules** This folder contains code modules, which are where you store your macros. A module can contain one or more macros. Word creates the NewMacros module automatically for you the first time you record a macro.
- **Class Modules** This folder contains classes, custom code objects you create. Classes are beyond the scope of this book.
- **References** (Documents only, not templates.) This folder contains a reference to the template attached to the document.

You can click the Toggle Folders button on the Project Window toolbar to display the list of objects not divided into folders. Click the button again to show the folders again.

The other two buttons on the Project Window toolbar—the View Code button and the View Object button—let you switch quickly between a userform itself (the object) and the code attached to it. You'll start using these buttons in Chapter 4.

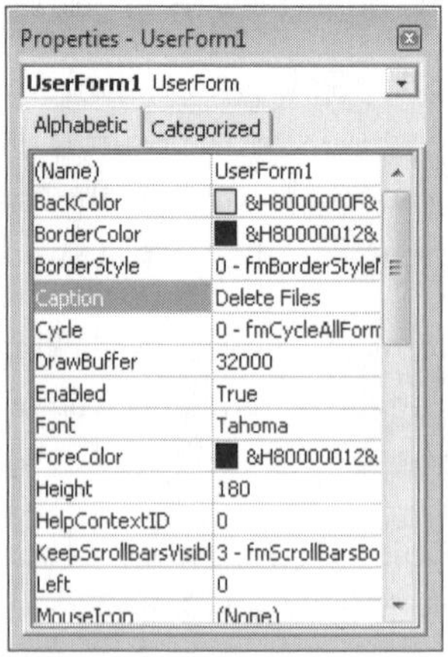

Figure 2-4 The Properties window lets you view and change properties for whichever object you've selected.

Understand the Properties Window

The Properties window (shown in Figure 2-4 with a userform selected) shows a list of the properties of the object you've currently selected. You can check the value of a property or (for most properties) change it. For example, the text you assign to the Caption property appears in the title bar of the form.

The Alphabetic tab shows an alphabetical list of the properties. The Categorized tab shows the same properties divided by category—Appearance, Behavior, Font, and so on.

Understand the Code Window

The Code window, which takes up the largest part of the Visual Basic Editor window, is where you create and edit your code. At the moment, the Code window should be displaying the code for the macro you recorded in Chapter 1.

At the lower-left corner of the Code window are two buttons:

■ **Procedure View**   Click this button to make the Code window show only one procedure at a time. Procedure view is useful when you're working on a single procedure.

■ **Full Module View**   Click this button to make the Code window show all the module's procedures. Full Module view is useful when you're working on multiple procedures within the same module.

You'll start working in the Code window later in this chapter and will see its helpful features in action.

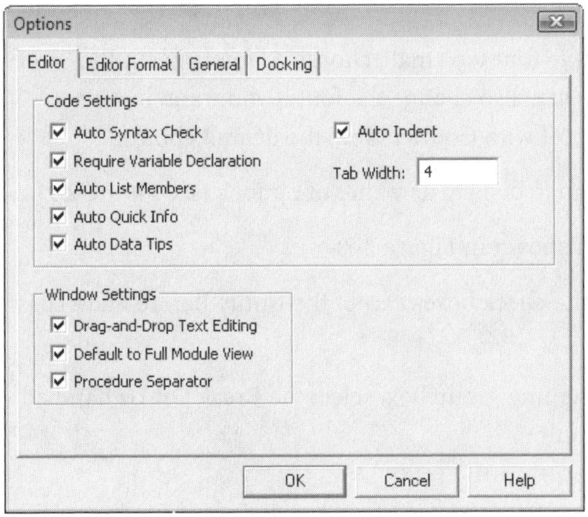

Figure 2-5   Make sure all the check boxes on the Editor tab of the Options dialog box are selected.

21

Configure the Visual Basic Editor So You Can Work Easily in It

Next, make sure the Visual Basic Editor is set up so that you can work easily in it. Follow these steps:

1. In the Visual Basic Editor, choose Tools | Options to open the Options dialog box, and then click the Editor tab if it's not already displayed. Figure 2-5 shows the Editor tab.

MEMO

We'll get into the details of these features later in this chapter and in the subsequent chapters. For now, simply choose the settings as instructed.

2. Make sure all of the check boxes are selected. You'll probably need to select the Require Variable Declaration check box, as VBA normally has this check box cleared at first.

3. Click the Editor Format tab to display its contents (see Figure 2-6).

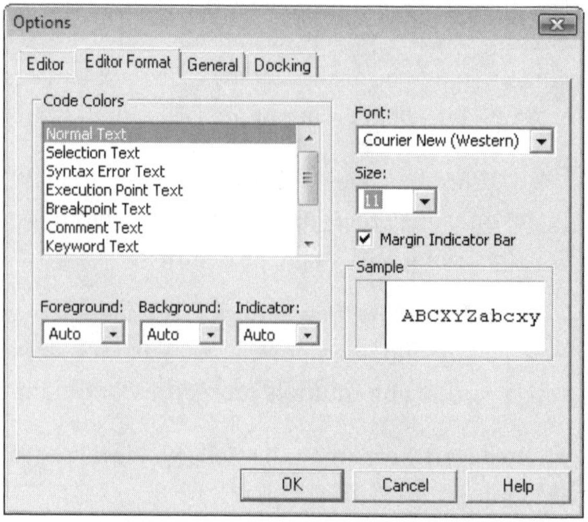

Figure 2-6 The Editor Format tab of the Options dialog box lets you change the font, font size, and color. At this point, just make sure the font size is easy to read.

MEMO

To make your code easier to read, VBA uses different colors for different categories of text: dark blue for keywords, green for comments, red for syntax errors, and so on. You'll read more about these shortly. The Editor Format tab of the Options dialog box lets you change the colors if you want. This book assumes that you're using the standard colors.

4. If you find the sample font too small, choose a larger size in the Size drop-down list. You can also change the font if you want, but it's usually best to start off with Courier New, the default choice.

5. Click the General tab to display its welter of options (see Figure 2-7).

6. Choose the settings shown in Figure 2-7:

- Select each of the check boxes except the Notify Before State Loss check box.

- In the Error Trapping group box, select the Break On Unhandled Errors option button.

22

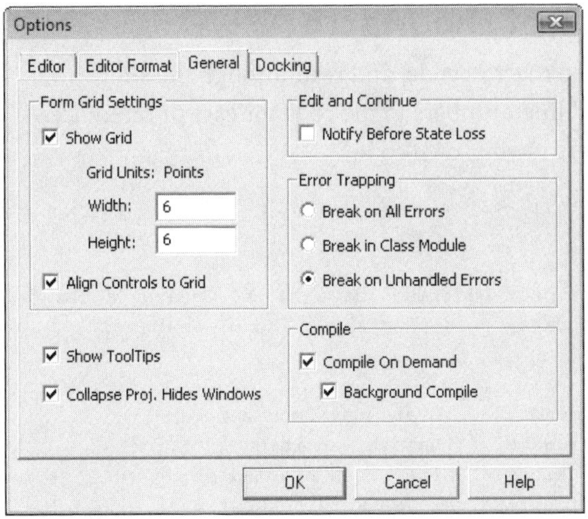

Options

Editor | Editor Format | General | Docking |

Form Grid Settings
☑ Show Grid

Grid Units: Points

Width: 6
Height: 6

☑ Align Controls to Grid

☑ Show ToolTips
☑ Collapse Proj. Hides Windows

Edit and Continue
☐ Notify Before State Loss

Error Trapping
○ Break on All Errors
○ Break in Class Module
◉ Break on Unhandled Errors

Compile
☑ Compile On Demand
☑ Background Compile

OK   Cancel   Help

Figure 2-7 Make sure the General tab of the Options dialog box is set up like this so that you can easily follow the examples in this book.

7. Click the Docking tab to display its list of dockable windows. *Dockable* means that you can *dock* (attach) a window to the Visual Basic Editor's window frame rather than having the window float freely.

8. Select the check box for each window except Object Browser.

9. Click the OK button to close the Options dialog box.

You're almost set to start editing. There's just one more thing to do—display the Edit toolbar and the Debug toolbar so that you have their controls available:

1. Right-click the menu bar, and then click Edit so that a check mark appears next to it and the Edit toolbar appears.

2. Right-click the menu bar again, and then click Debug, again placing a check mark next to it and displaying the Debug toolbar.

3. If either of the toolbars is floating free, double-click its title bar to dock it.

4. Drag the toolbars so that they're conveniently arranged at the top of the Visual Basic Editor window.

Examine the Macro You Recorded

Now that you've set up the Visual Basic Editor, you're ready to examine the macro you've recorded. The best way to do this is to *step through* the macro, executing one code statement at a time and watching what happens.

If you've looked
at programming
languages such as C
or C++, you may be
pleasantly surprised
to find how easy VBA
is to read. You'll also
notice that the code
lines are indented
to different levels
to make it easier to
read and to show
where a statement
has been continued
to a second or
subsequent line.

Look at the Code of the Macro

First, take a quick look at the macro's code, and read through the short
explanation of it. I've added line numbers to the code for ease of reference.
You won't see these numbers in your own code.

```
1.   Sub WMME_Transfer_Data()
2.   '
3.   ' WMME_Transfer_Data Macro
4.   ' Opens Latest Report.docx and finds data in it. Creates a new
     document, copies the data to it, and saves and closes
     the document.
5.   '
6.       ChangeFileOpenDirectory "C:\Users\Ken\Documents\WMME\"
7.       Documents.Open FileName:="""Latest Report.docx""", _
             ConfirmConversions:= False, ReadOnly:=False, _
             AddToRecentFiles:=False, PasswordDocument:="", _
             PasswordTemplate:="", Revert:=False, _
             WritePasswordDocument:="", WritePasswordTemplate:="", _
             Format:=wdOpenFormatAuto, XMLTransform:=""
8.       Selection.MoveDown Unit:=wdParagraph, Count:=1
9.       Selection.MoveDown Unit:=wdParagraph, Count:=1,
             Extend:=wdExtend
10.      Selection.Copy
11.      ActiveWindow.Close
12.      Documents.Add DocumentType:=wdNewBlankDocument
13.      Selection.Style = ActiveDocument.Styles("Heading 1")
14.      Selection.TypeText Text:="Report Summary"
15.      Selection.TypeParagraph
16.      Selection.PasteAndFormat (wdPasteDefault)
17.      ActiveDocument.SaveAs FileName:="Report Summary.docx", _
             FileFormat:=wdFormatXMLDocument, LockComments:=False, _
             Password:="", AddToRecentFiles:=True, WritePassword:="",_
             ReadOnlyRecommended:=False, EmbedTrueTypeFonts :=False, _
             SaveNativePictureFormat:=False, _
             SaveFormsData:=False, SaveAsAOCELetter:=False
18.      ActiveWindow.Close
19. End Sub
```

MEMO

A *subprocedure* is one of the two types of code unit you normally create with VBA. The other type of code unit is a *function*, which begins with a Function statement and ends with an End Function statement.

MEMO

You'll notice that line 7 is actually six lines of code: The Visual Basic Editor has automatically broken it onto extra lines to stop the lines from becoming unreadably long. To break a line of code, you put a space followed by an underscore, as on these lines. You can break a line between any keywords or values, so you can use line breaks freely to make your code easier to read.

I'll give you the details of what objects, collections, properties, methods, and arguments are in a moment, but here's what happens in the code:

- The Sub statement in line 1 starts the subprocedure, and the End Sub statement in line 19 ends it.

- After the Sub statement come four lines of comments. A *comment* is a line of code that you tell VBA to ignore, either because you don't want to use a particular statement at the moment or because you want to add comments to explain your code to yourself or other programmers. You put an apostrophe before any code on the line that you want VBA to ignore. Here, the apostrophe appears at the beginning of each line, so the whole of each line is commented out. However, you can also comment out only part of a line.

- Line 6 uses the ChangeFileOpenDirectory command to change the folder (directory) that appears in the Open dialog box.

- Line 7 uses the Open method of the Documents collection to open the Latest Report.docx document. FileName is the key argument here; don't worry about the other arguments for the moment.

- Line 8 uses the MoveDown method of the Selection object to move the current selection down one paragraph. The Selection object represents the current selection, whether it's an insertion point (with no content), a selection that contains words or characters, or another object (for example, a picture).

- Line 9 uses the MoveDown method of the Selection object again, but this time with the Extend:=wdExtend argument. This makes Word select from the selection's current position to the end of the paragraph.

- Line 10 uses the Copy method of the Selection object to copy the selection to the Clipboard.

- Line 11 uses the Close method of the ActiveWindow object to close the active window.

- Line 12 uses the Add method of the Documents collection to add a Document object. The DocumentType argument specifies that it's a blank document (wdNewBlankDocument).

- Line 13 sets the Style property of the Selection object to the style named "Heading 1" in the active document.

- Line 14 uses the TypeText method of the Selection object to type the text "Report Summary."

- Line 15 uses the TypeParagraph method of the Selection object to "type" a paragraph (the equivalent of you pressing ENTER at the end of a paragraph).

- Line 16 uses the PasteAndFormat method of the Selection object to paste in the text from the Clipboard. VBA lets you paste in different ways just as Word does—for example, pasting styled text, or text free of formatting. This time, we use default paste behavior—wdPasteDefault in VBA terms.

- Line 17 uses the SaveAs method of the ActiveDocument object to save the document. There's a whole welter of arguments here, but for now look only as far as the FileName argument (which specifies the filename) and the FileFormat argument (which specifies the file format to use). Chapter 12 explains the rest of the most useful arguments.

- Line 18 uses the Close method of the ActiveWindow object to close the active window (and thus close the document).

- Line 19 simply ends the macro (as noted earlier).

UNDERSTAND KEY VBA TERMS

Here are six key terms you'll need to know for working with VBA:

- An *object* is an item such as a document (the Document object), a window (the Window object), or a selection (the Selection object). An object can have properties, methods, or both.

- A *collection* is a group of objects of the same type. For example, the Documents collection contains all the open Document objects—a collection's name is usually the plural of the object's name, as in this case, but there are some exceptions.

- A *property* is an attribute of an object that you can set. For example, the Style property of the Selection object controls the style applied to the selection. Style is a *read-write* property, so you can both find out what style is currently applied and apply a different style. Some properties are *read-only*: you can find out their current settings, but you cannot change them.

- A *method* is an action you can take with (or on) an object or collection. For example, the Open method of the Documents collection opens a document.

- An *argument* is a piece of information you provide to a method to tell it what to do. For example, when you use the Open method of the Documents collection to open a document, you must use the FileName argument to tell VBA the name of the file to open. Some arguments are required (always needed), as FileName is here, while others are optional.

- A *variable* is a storage slot you create for storing information temporarily in a macro.

27

Step into the Macro

Now that you've read what the macro does, try stepping into it so that you can see it in action. *Step into* means to go through the macro one command at a time, watching what each command does.

To step through your macro, follow these steps:

1. Arrange the Visual Basic Editor window and the Word window so that you can see both. The easiest way is to minimize all other windows except these two, right-click the system clock, and then choose Show Windows Side By Side.

2. Press ALT-F11 to move the focus to the Visual Basic Editor window.

3. Click in the WMME_Transfer_Data macro.

4. Press F8, or click the Step
   Into button on the Debug
   toolbar as shown here,
   to start stepping into the
   macro.

5. The Visual Basic Editor
   highlights the macro's Sub
   statement and places an arrow
   next to it.

```
⇨   Sub WMME_Transfer_Data()
    '
    ' WMME_Transfer_Data Macro
```

6. Press F8 or click the Step Into button again. Notice that the Visual
   Basic Editor skips over the four comment lines and highlights the
   ChangeFileOpenDirectory line.

7. Press F8 or click the Step Into button again. The Visual Basic Editor
   executes the ChangeFileOpenDirectory statement, but this has no
   visible effect, so you see no change. The Visual Basic Editor highlights
   the Documents.Open statement.

8. Press F8 or click the Step Into button to execute the Documents.Open
   statement. The Latest Report.docx document opens in the Word window.

9. Continue pressing F8 (or clicking the Step Into button) and watching
   the actions that take place. When you execute the End Sub statement,
   the macro ends.

Edit the Macro

In this section, you'll make some easy edits to the macro that change what it
does. As you edit the macro, you'll see some of the Visual Basic Editor's most
important code-completion features in action.

UNDERSTAND THE OPTION EXPLICIT STATEMENT

The Option Explicit statement tells VBA to force you to make a formal declaration of each variable you use in your code. These declarations help you avoid confusion with variables and variable types.

After you select the Require Variable Declaration check box on the Editor tab of the Options dialog box, VBA automatically adds this statement to each new Code sheet you create. However, because the NewMacros module exists already, you need to add the Option Explicit statement to its Code sheet manually.

Add an Option Explicit Statement if Necessary

First, look at the top of the Code window to see if there's an Option Explicit statement. If not (as is most likely), click before the first line of code, type **option explicit** (in lowercase), and press ENTER.

Notice that the Visual Basic Editor automatically applies title case when you press ENTER: whenever you end a line of code, the Visual Basic Editor checks it to make sure that it doesn't contain any immediately identifiable errors.

See the Visual Basic Editor Identify a Compile Error

Now watch what happens when you enter a line of code that doesn't compile correctly.

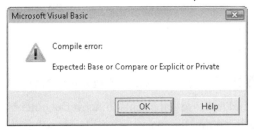

On the line below Option Explicit, type **option implicit** and press ENTER. This isn't proper VBA code, so the Visual Basic Editor displays a Compile Error message box like the one shown here. (The message means that you can use Option Base, Option Compare, Option Explicit, and Option Private statements.)

Click the OK button to close the message box, and then delete the "option implicit" statement. The easiest way to do this is to move the mouse pointer into the selection bar just to the left of the line so that it turns into an arrow pointing up and to the right, click once to select the whole line, and then press DELETE.

Now it's time for you to make some changes to the macro.

29

> You can use many standard editing commands from Word and other text editors in the Visual Basic Editor as well. Better yet, it has powerful code-completion features that you'll meet shortly.

Remove the ChangeFileOpenDirectory Statement

Having the ChangeFileOpenDirectory statement at the beginning of the macro isn't great, because it means that you (or whoever runs the macro) will see the WMME folder the next time you display the Open dialog box.

Instead, it's better to put the full path and filename in the Documents .Open statement. Follow these steps:

1. In the ChangeFileOpenDirectory line, select the file path—for example, **C:\Users\Ken\Documents\WMME**. Don't select the double quotation marks.

2. Press CTRL-C or click the Copy button on the Standard toolbar to copy the path to the Clipboard.

3. In the Documents.Open line, click to position the insertion point just before Latest Report.docx (after the double quotation marks).

4. Press CTRL-V or click the Paste button on the Standard toolbar to paste in the path.

5. In the Documents.SaveAs line, click to position the insertion point before Report Summary.docx (after the double quotation marks), and then paste in the path.

6. Select the ChangeFileOpenDirectory line, and then delete it.

Replace the ActiveWindow.Close Statements

Now, let's change the two ActiveWindow.Close statements to ActiveDocument .Close statements. You can do this by editing the macro manually, but using Find and Replace is even quicker. Follow these steps:

1. Choose Edit | Replace or press CTRL-H to display the Replace dialog box (see Figure 2-8).

2. Type **ActiveWindow.Close** in the Find What box.

Replace

Find What:	ActiveWindow.Close ▾
Replace With:	activedocument.close| ▾

Search
- ○ Current Procedure
- ● Current Module
- ○ Current Project
- ○ Selected Text

Direction: All ▾

☐ Find Whole Word Only
☐ Match Case
☐ Use Pattern Matching

Find Next
Cancel
Replace
Replace All
Help

Figure 2-8   You can use the Visual Basic Editor's full-functioned Replace feature to change your code quickly. You can let the Visual Basic Editor handle the capitalization for you.

3. Type **activedocument.close** in the Replace With box.

4. Click the Replace All button. The Visual Basic Editor tells you how many replacements it has made:

Microsoft Visual Basic

ℹ The specified region has been searched. 2 replacements were made.

OK   Help

5. Click the OK button to close the Microsoft Visual Basic dialog box.

6. Click the Cancel button or press ESC to close the Replace dialog box.

Add Further Statements to the Macro

Now add further statements to the macro to change what it does. Follow these steps:

1. Click at the end of the Selection.TypeText line, and then press ENTER to create a new line. Notice that the Visual Basic Editor starts the new line at the same level of indentation as the previous line.

2. Type **sel** and then press CTRL-SPACEBAR. This is the keyboard shortcut for the Complete Word feature. Notice that the Visual Basic Editor automatically completes the word **Selection** for you (and capitalizes the first letter).

3. Type a period after Selection. The Visual Basic Editor displays the available properties and methods for the Selection object, as shown here. This feature is called List Properties/Methods.

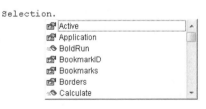

Selection.
- Active
- Application
- BoldRun
- BookmarkID
- Bookmarks
- Borders
- Calculate

4. Type **typet** to scroll down quickly to the TypeText method, and then press TAB to enter the method in your code.

5. Press SPACEBAR to type a space. The Visual Basic Editor displays the argument list, showing each argument and its type. As you can see here, the TypeText method takes only one argument, Text, and its type is String.

```
Selection.TypeText |
          TypeText(Text As String)
```

6. Type the argument, a colon, an equal sign, and then the text you want to "type":

```
Selection.TypeText Text:="Here is the latest report
summary."
```

7. Select the Selection.TypeParagraph line (click in the selection bar at the left edge of the Code window) and then CTRL-drag it up to the beginning of the second Selection.TypeText paragraph, as shown here (the gray vertical bar to the left of the mouse pointer indicates where the dragged item will land). As in Word, CTRL-dragging copies the selection rather than moving it.

```
Selection.Style = ActiveDocument.Styles("Heading 1")
Selection.TypeText Text:="Report Summary"
Selection.TypeText Text:="Here is the latest report :
Selection.TypeParagraph
Selection.PasteAndFormat (wdPasteDefault)
```

8. Click at the beginning of the ActiveDocument.Close statement at the end of the macro, and then type an apostrophe to comment out the line:

```
'ActiveDocument.Close
```

9. When you move the insertion point to another line, notice that the Visual Basic Editor turns the commented line green.

After these edits, your macro should look like this (including the Option Explicit statement that precedes the macro):

```
Option Explicit

Sub WMME_Transfer_Data()
'
' WMME_Transfer_Data Macro
' Opens Latest Report.docx and finds data in it. Creates a new
document, copies the data to it, and saves and closes the document.
'
    Documents.Open FileName:= _
        "C:\Users\Ken\Documents\WMME\Latest Report.docx", _
        ConfirmConversions:=False, ReadOnly:=False, _
        AddToRecentFiles:=False, PasswordDocument:="", _
        PasswordTemplate:="", Revert:=False, _
        WritePasswordDocument:="", WritePasswordTemplate:="", _
        Format:=wdOpenFormatAuto, XMLTransform:=""
    Selection.MoveDown Unit:=wdParagraph, Count:=1
    Selection.MoveDown Unit:=wdParagraph, Count:=1, Extend:=wdExtend
    Selection.Copy
    ActiveDocument.Close
    Documents.Add DocumentType:=wdNewBlankDocument
    Selection.Style = ActiveDocument.Styles("Heading 1")
    Selection.TypeText Text:="Report Summary"
    Selection.TypeParagraph
    Selection.TypeText Text:="Here is the latest report summary:"
    Selection.TypeParagraph
    Selection.PasteAndFormat (wdPasteDefault)
    ActiveDocument.SaveAs FileName:= _
        "C:\Users\Ken\Documents\WMME\Report Summary.docx", FileFormat:= _
        wdFormatXMLDocument, LockComments:=False, Password:="", _
        AddToRecentFiles:=True, WritePassword:="", _
        ReadOnlyRecommended:=False, EmbedTrueTypeFonts _
        :=False, SaveNativePictureFormat:=False, SaveFormsData:=False, _
        SaveAsAOCELetter:=False
    ActiveDocument.Close
End Sub
```

Run the Edited Macro

Now run the edited version of the macro. To do so, simply click in it and then either click the Run Sub/UserForm button on the Standard toolbar or the Debug toolbar (the button appears on both toolbars) or press F5. The macro runs at full speed, rather than one command at a time.

Because you've commented out the final ActiveDocument.Close statement, the Report Summary.docx document remains open, so you can see the effect of the changes you've made: the report contains the extra paragraph with the text you typed into your code.

Save Your Changes and Quit Word

Now remove the comment from your macro, save your changes, and quit Word. Follow these steps:

1. In the Visual Basic Editor, delete the apostrophe from the start of the second ActiveDocument.Close line. Move the insertion point to another line, and you'll see the line change from the green of comments to the regular colors for code statements.

2. Click the Save button on the Standard toolbar or press CTRL-S to save changes to the Normal template.

3. Choose File | Close And Return to Microsoft Word or press ALT-Q to close the Visual Basic Editor and return to the Word window.

4. Close the Report Summary.docx document and quit Word by clicking the Microsoft Office button and then clicking Exit Word.

Control a Macro with Message Boxes and Input Boxes

One of the easiest ways of making your macros more useful and powerful is to let the user control them.

In this chapter, you'll learn how to use message boxes—simple dialog boxes—to let the user make decisions as a macro runs, and how to use input boxes to let the user provide text input. You'll work with message boxes and input boxes by attaching them to the macro you recorded in Chapter 1 and edited in Chapter 2.

In the next chapter, you'll see how to create your own custom dialog boxes to allow the user to interact with your macros in more complex ways. And Chapter 14 shows you how to summon up Word's built-in dialog boxes for use in your macros.

Add Message Boxes to Your Macro

A *message box* is a small, standardized dialog box that contains only a few elements:

- A title bar containing the program's name or general information

- The text of the message you want to convey to the user

- An icon to indicate which category of message it is—a question, information, an alert, or a warning

- One, two, three, or four buttons that allow the user to choose what to do (or simply close the message box)

Figure 3-1 shows an example of a two-button message box with a Yes button and a No button. There's nothing to it—but it's great for making decisions in your code.

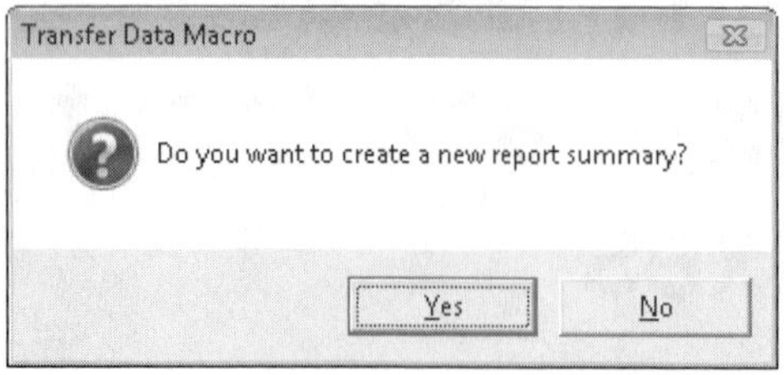

Transfer Data Macro

Do you want to create a new report summary?

Yes   No

Figure 3-1   A two-button message box is great for confirming that the user actually intends to run the macro they've started—and that they know what the macro will do.

Get Ready to Work Through This Chapter

Before we can get started with message boxes and input boxes, you need to set up the Visual Basic Editor ready for working and create a copy of the module containing the macro you'll be adapting.

Open the Visual Basic Editor and the Macro

Follow these steps to open the Visual Basic Editor and the macro:

1. Open Microsoft Word if it's not already running.

2. Click the Developer tab, go to the Code group, and then click Visual Basic to open the Visual Basic Editor.

3. If the Code window for the WMME_Chapter_1 code module opens, you're all set. If not, choose Tools | Macros to open the Macros dialog box in the Visual Basic Editor (see Figure 3-2).

4. In the Macro Name list, click the WMME_Transfer_Data macro, and then click the Edit button. The Visual Basic Editor opens the code module containing the macro.

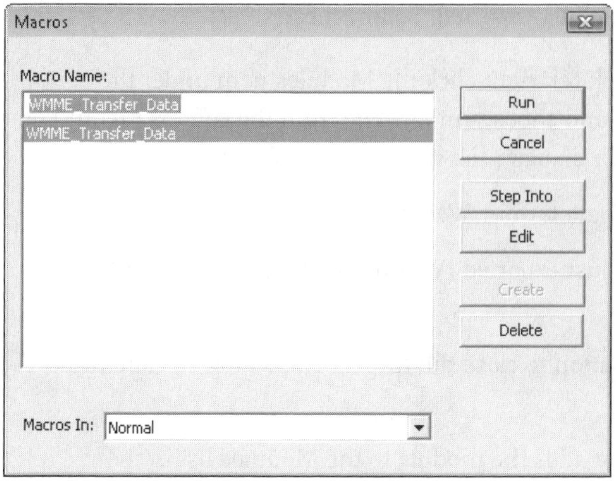

Figure 3-2   You can use the Macros dialog box in the Visual Basic Editor to navigate quickly to the code module containing a particular macro.

Create a Copy of the Module

Now create a copy of the code module so that you can work with a copy of the code. The easiest way to do this is to export the WMME_Chapter_1 code module to a file, and then immediately import that file.

Follow these steps to export the file:

1. In the Project Explorer window, right-click the WMME_Chapter_1 module and choose Export File from the context menu. The Visual Basic Editor displays the Export File dialog box (see Figure 3-3).

2. Navigate to the WMME folder you created in your Documents folder (on Windows Vista) or your My Documents folder (on Windows XP).

3. Accept the default filename, WMME_Chapter_1.bas (if you've set Windows to display file extensions) or WMME_Chapter_1 (if Windows is hiding file extensions).

4. Click the Save button to close the Export File dialog box and save the file.

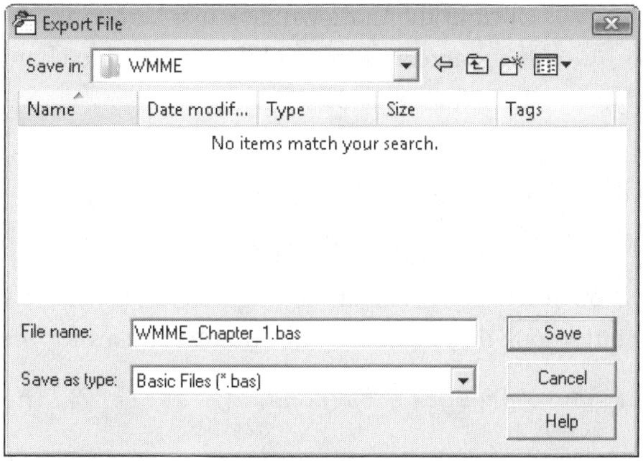

37

Figure 3-3   Use the Export File dialog box to export a code module (or other module) to a file for safe keeping or so that you can import it elsewhere.

MEMO

The Visual Basic Editor saves code modules using the .bas file extension, which Windows associates with the Basic Files file type. (This is "Basic Files" in the sense of "Visual Basic files" rather than "simple files.")

Now import the file you just exported. Follow these steps:

1. In the Project Explorer, right-click the Modules item under the Normal template and choose Import File from the context menu. The Visual Basic Editor displays the Import File dialog box.

2. If necessary, navigate to your WMME folder.

3. Click the file you just exported (WMME_Chapter_1.bas or WMME_Chapter_1).

4. Click the Open button to close the Import File dialog box and import the module.

The Visual Basic Editor adds the module to the Modules list in the Normal template. You'll see that the Visual Basic Editor renames the module to WMME_Chapter_11 (adding a second 1 at the end) to make its name different from that of the existing module.

Rename the module and the macro like this:

1. Click the WMME_Chapter_11 module in the Project Explorer.

2. Click in the Properties window at the end of the (Name) field.

3. Edit the name to WMME_Chapter_3, and then press ENTER.

4. Click in the Code window just before the parenthesis at the end of the macro's name, and then type _3 to change the name to WMME_Transfer_Data_3.

Understand the Basic Syntax for Message Boxes

Now you're ready to start adding message boxes to the macro. First, have a quick look through the syntax that VBA uses for message boxes:

```
MsgBox(prompt[, buttons] [, title] [, helpfile, context])
```

That looks confusing with all the brackets and commas. Here's what it means:

- MsgBox is VBA's function for displaying a message box. Normally, you put the arguments in parentheses, as shown here, so that you can check the result of the message box and find out which button the user clicked.

- *prompt* is the only required argument. This is the text string containing the text you want to display in the message box. The text can be up to 1,024 characters long.

- *buttons* is an optional argument that controls which buttons and which icon the message box contains. If you omit *buttons*, you get an OK-only message box with no icon, so usually you'll want to use *buttons*. I'll give you the details in a minute.

- *title* is an optional argument that supplies the text to display in the title bar of the message box—for example, the name of the macro that's running. Usually, you'll want to specify *title* to help the user grasp the message box's meaning and importance. If you omit *title*, VBA puts "Microsoft Word" in the title bar so that the user at least knows which program the message box belongs to. You can make about 75 characters appear in the title bar—any more than that, and VBA truncates the title—but having a shorter title bar is usually a better idea.

- *helpfile* is an optional argument that tells Windows which help file to open if the user clicks the Help button in the message box. If you specify *helpfile*, you must also specify *context*, which tells Windows which topic in the help file to display. Unless you create your own help files, you probably won't need to use these arguments, so I won't give examples of them in this chapter.

Understand the buttons Argument

To tell VBA which command buttons and icons to display in the message box, you specify the appropriate value or constant for the *buttons* argument.

Here are the values and constants that control the command buttons:

Buttons	Constant	Value
OK	vbOKOnly	0
OK, Cancel	vbOKCancel	1
Abort, Retry, Ignore	vbAbortRetryIgnore	2
Yes, No, Cancel	vbYesNoCancel	3
Yes, No	vbYesNo	4
Retry, Cancel	vbRetryCancel	5

The second part of the *buttons* argument tells VBA which icon to include in the message box. Here are the values and constants that control the icon:

Icon	Constant	Value
Stop icon	vbCritical	16
Question-mark icon	vbQuestion	32
Exclamation-point icon	vbExclamation	48
Information icon	vbInformation	64

There's one more part to the *buttons* argument: setting the default button. You'll need to do this only when you need to override VBA's habit of making the first button the default button. For example, in a Yes/No message box, the Yes button is the default button—but if you expect the answer to be No, you can set the No button to be the default button. That way, if someone simply presses ENTER to dismiss the message box, they choose the No button rather than the Yes button.

To set the default button, use the constants or values shown here:

Default Button	Constant	Value
First button	vbDefaultButton1	0
Second button	vbDefaultButton2	256
Third button	vbDefaultButton3	512
Fourth button	vbDefaultButton4	768

To set the default button, you add it to the first parts of the *buttons* argument by using a plus sign, like this:

```
If MsgBox("Create a new document?", vbYesNo + vbQuestion + _
    vbDefaultButton2, "Create New Document") = vbYes
    Then Documents.Add
```

Put Message Boxes into Action

After all that theory, try adding two message boxes to the macro you recorded in Chapter 1, edited in Chapter 2, and renamed to WMME_Transfer_Data_3 at the beginning of this chapter.

Add the First Message Box

To add a message box, follow these steps:

1. Click at the beginning of the Documents.Open line, press ENTER to create a new line, and then press UP ARROW to move back to the new line.

2. Type **If MsgBox(** to start a MsgBox statement preceded by an If condition. The Visual Basic Editor displays a ScreenTip with the syntax for the MsgBox function, as shown here. The Prompt argument is in bold, indicating this is the next argument.

```
If MsgBox(
    MsgBox(Prompt, [Buttons As VbMsgBoxStyle = vbOKOnly], [Title], [HelpFile], [Context]) As VbMsgBoxResult
```

3. Type the prompt for the message box:

    `"Create a new report summary?"`

4. Type a comma. The Visual Basic Editor displays a ScreenTip with the next argument, Buttons, in bold, and displays the list of available options:

```
If MsgBox("Create a new report summary?",|
    MsgBox(Prompt, [Buttons As VbMsgBoxStyle = vbOKOnly], [Title], [HelpFile], [Context]) As VbMsgBoxResult
```
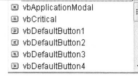

vbApplicationModal
vbCritical
vbDefaultButton1
vbDefaultButton2
vbDefaultButton3
vbDefaultButton4

42

5. Type **vby** to select the vbYesNo item in the list, and then press TAB to enter it.

6. Type a space and a plus sign (+). The Visual Basic Editor displays the list of options for completing the Buttons argument again.

7. Type **vbq** to select the vbQuestion item in the list, and then press COMMA to enter it and move along to the next part of the statement:

```
If MsgBox("Create a new report summary?",vbYesNo +vbQuestion,
    MsgBox(Prompt, [Buttons As VbMsgBoxStyle = vbOKOnly], [Title], [HelpFile], [Context]) As VbMsgBoxResult
```

8. Type **"Transfer Data Macro"** (including the double quotation marks) as the title for the message box, and then type **)**, a closing parenthesis. The Visual Basic Editor hides the ScreenTip.

9. Type a space and **= vbYes Then** to complete the If statement for the message box.

10. Move to the end of the macro and click just after the ActiveDocument .Close statement.

11. Press ENTER to create a new line, and then type **end if** on that line. When you move the insertion point from the line, the Visual Basic Editor applies initial caps, making the statement End If.

12. Select all the text from the Documents.Open statement near the beginning of the macro to the ActiveDocument.Close statement near the end.

13. Press TAB or click the Indent button on the Edit toolbar (as shown here) to indent the code by one tab stop. This indentation makes the hierarchy of the code clearer: All the code between the If statement and the End If statement is conditional on the If statement evaluating to True. If the user clicks the No button, VBA goes from the If line to the End If line, and then the macro ends.

14. Press CTRL-S or click the Save button on the Standard toolbar to save the changes.

Test the First Message Box

Now test the first message box:

1. Click in the macro, and then press F8 three times to step through to the MsgBox line. The Visual Basic Editor displays the message box, as shown on the right.

2. Click the No button or press ESC. The message box closes and the highlight jumps to the End If line.

3. Press F8 twice more to execute the End If statement and then the End Sub statement.

43

4. Click in the macro again, but this time press F5. The message box appears.

5. Click the Yes button. The macro runs, opening the Latest Report.docx document, creating the summary document, and then closing both documents.

Add and Test the Second Message Box

Now add a second message box to the end of the macro. This message box contains only an OK button, so you don't need to retrieve which button the user clicks—there's only one choice.

Follow these steps:

1. Click at the end of the ActiveDocument.Close statement, and then press ENTER to create a new line.

2. Type the following MsgBox statement, breaking it with an underscore (after a space) for practice:

```
MsgBox "The macro has created the report summary.", _
    vbOKOnly + vbInformation, "Transfer Data Macro"
```

3. Press F5 to run the macro, and then click the Yes button in the first message box. The macro runs as before, and then the second message box appears, as shown here.

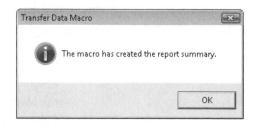

4. Click the OK button to close the second message box, and then the macro finishes.

5. Press CTRL-S or click the Save button on the Standard toolbar to save the changes.

USING MULTI-BUTTON MESSAGE BOXES

So far, you've seen VBA's two most useful message boxes: a Yes/No message box, and an OK-only message box. As you read earlier in this chapter, VBA also offers an OK/Cancel message box and a Retry/Cancel message box. You can use these in exactly the same way as the Yes/No message box.

With a two-button message box, you need check only whether one of the buttons was clicked: if it wasn't clicked, the other button was. To make this check, you can use an If… Then condition as shown in this chapter.

In some cases, you may not need to take any action for one of the buttons. For example, in the Transfer_Data_3 macro, clicking the Yes button in the Yes/No message box runs the code; clicking No simply doesn't run it. In other cases, you may need to write separate code for the second button, using an If… Then… Else… statement (discussed in Chapter 6).

VBA also offers two three-button message boxes: Yes/No/Cancel, and Abort/Retry/Ignore. A Yes/No/Cancel message box can be useful for occasions when you need to let the user stop the running macro (with the Cancel button) as well as make a decision about the question you're raising. An Abort/Retry/Ignore message box is seldom useful, as the terminology tends to confuse the user.

You can also add a Help button to any message box, so you may need to check up to four buttons.

To find out which button the user clicked in a three-button message box, use an If… Then… ElseIf… Else statement. For a four-button message box (including a Help button), use an If… Then… ElseIf… ElseIf… Else statement.

45

CREATING MULTIPLE LINES OF TEXT IN A MESSAGE BOX

You can use up to 1,024 characters in the prompt of a message box, which is enough for around 150 words—but don't expect most users to read a message this long.

All the text appears in a single paragraph unless you break it up by using a carriage-return character (vbCr) to break a line. By using two carriage returns, you can create paragraphs separated by a blank line. This can make a longer message far easier to read.

For example, try changing the MsgBox statement at the end of your macro so that it looks like this:

```
MsgBox "The macro has created the report
summary." & vbCr & vbCr _
```

```
    & "The report summary is in Report
Summary.docx", _
    vbOKOnly + vbInformation, "Transfer
Data Macro"
```

When you run the macro, you see a message box like that shown here:

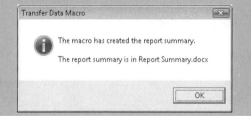

An input box is a
great way of having
the user input a
single piece of
information to a
macro. You can
easily use multiple
input boxes in
sequence to gather
several pieces of
information, but
users will often
find the macro
awkward to use.
A custom dialog
box (discussed in
the next chapter)
is usually an easier
means of gathering
multiple pieces of
information.

Add an Input Box

An *input box* is a standardized message box with two buttons (OK and Cancel)
that contains a single text field in which the user can enter text. You can use
an input box to request user input or to prompt the user to accept or change a
default value. Figure 3-4 shows a typical input box.

Figure 3-4   An input box
is a simple dialog box that
contains a single text field and
OK and Cancel buttons.

Understand the Syntax for Input Boxes

To display an input box, you use this syntax:

```
InputBox(prompt[, title] [, default] [, xpos] [, ypos]
[, helpfile, context]
```

Most of these arguments are the same as for message boxes. Here's an
executive summary, but look back to earlier in the chapter for full details:

- *prompt* is the message text that appears in the input box telling the user
  what to do. This is the only required argument.

- *title* is the title of the input box. Usually you'll want to specify this
  argument so that your input boxes don't say "Microsoft Word" in the
  title bar.

- *default* is the text you want to display in the text field, either as a default
  value (if the user doesn't change it) or as an example of the kind of
  input you want. Depending on what input the input box is seeking,
  default text is sometimes helpful but other times unhelpful. If you
  need to force the user to enter text, leave *default* blank so that you can
  check the user's input.

- *xpos* and *ypos* are numeric values that let you control where the input box appears on the screen. The numbers are in twips (a *twip*, short for a twentieth of an inch point, is 1/1440 inch). Because twips vary depending on screen resolution, it's normally best to omit *xpos* and *ypos* so that VBA displays the input box in the default position: halfway across the screen, and two-thirds of the way up it.

- *helpfile* specifies the help file to use if the user clicks the Help button, and *context* specifies the help topic within the help file. Unless you develop your own help files (which is beyond the scope of this book), you probably won't want to use these arguments.

Add the Input Box to the Macro

You're now ready to add the input box to the macro. Follow these steps:

1. Go to the Selection.TypeText Text:="Report Summary" line and select the "Report Summary" part (including the double quotation marks).

2. Over the selected text (replacing it), type **inputbox(**. The Visual Basic Editor displays the ScreenTip showing the arguments and highlights the Prompt argument:

```
Selection.TypeText Text:=inputbox(|
                        InputBox(Prompt, [Title], [Default], [XPos], [YPos],
                        [HelpFile], [Context]) As String
```

3. Type the rest of the statement, this time spelling out each argument you're using. Put the argument's name, a colon, an equal sign, and then the value in double quotation marks, as shown here:

```
Selection.TypeText Text:=InputBox( _
    Prompt:="Type the title here:", _
    Title:="Transfer Data Macro", _
    Default:="Report Summary")
```

4. Comment out the ActiveDocument.Close statement at the end of the macro by typing an apostrophe (') at the beginning of the line.

THE EASY WAY

As you type the InputBox statement, notice that the ScreenTip doesn't show the next argument in bold when you type a comma after assigning a value to the previous argument. Instead, the ScreenTip shows an argument in bold when you type its name followed by a colon. This is because, when you use the argument names, you can provide the arguments out of order if you want to. By contrast, when you don't use the argument names, you must use the arguments in the order that VBA expects.

For this input box, it doesn't matter what kind of input you provide: whatever you type in the input box, the Selection .TypeText statement enters in the document. But for other input boxes, you may need to check that the input is of the right type. For example, if you display an input box to let the user specify how many folders to create, and the user types **sausage** instead of a number, your code will run into problems. You'll learn how to check the user's input later in this book.

Test the Input Box

Now test the input box:

1. Run your macro as usual. For example, click in it, and then click the Run Sub/UserForm button.

2. Click the Yes button in the first message box.

3. When the input box appears, type the text of your choice over the default text, and then press ENTER or click the OK button.

4. After you dismiss the second message box, look at the Report Summary.docx document to make sure that the text you typed appears in the first paragraph.

Try running the macro again but this time clicking the Cancel button in the input box. Notice that you get a blank paragraph this time. This is because clicking the Cancel button causes the input box to return what's called an *empty string*—a string of text that contains no characters.

Save Your Work

Follow these steps to finish up for the chapter:

1. Close the Report Summary.docx document manually (for example, press ALT, F, C in sequence).

2. Press ALT-F11 to switch to the Visual Basic Editor.

3. Delete the comma at the beginning of the second ActiveDocument .Close statement.

4. Press CTRL-S to save the changes you've made to the Normal template.

5. Press ALT-Q to close the Visual Basic Editor and return to Word.

Create a Custom Dialog Box

As you saw in the previous chapter, message boxes and input boxes provide a quick and easy way to let users interact with your macros.

But often you'll need greater interaction than message boxes and input boxes can easily provide. In this case, you can create a custom dialog box containing check boxes, option buttons, text boxes, command buttons, and other controls. This takes some time and effort but is highly effective and can make a macro look very professional—even if most of what the macro does is code you recorded with the Macro Recorder.

This chapter explains all the controls you can use in dialog boxes and shows you how to build a dialog box onto the macro you've been working with so far in this book.

Understand What You'll Do in This Chapter

In VBA, you create a custom dialog box by placing controls on a blank sheet called a *userform*. You then add code to the userform to run the userform itself and the controls it contains.

Transfer Data Macro

1. Choose the Source Document

Source Document:

Latest Report.docx

2. Choose the Data to Transfer
- Transfer All Data
- Transfer Only Key Data

3. Choose Options
Type the Title of the Document:

Report Summary

☑ Close the New Document

OK   Cancel

Figure 4-1 The custom dialog box you will create in this chapter adds flexibility and power to the macro you have recorded and edited.

MEMO

Make sure the Properties window Alphabetic tab is at the front rather than the Categorized tab. If the Categorized tab is at the front, the properties appear in different locations from those described here.

Figure 4-1 shows the custom dialog box that you will create in this chapter. It looks complex, but you can have it up and running in less than half an hour.

The custom dialog box makes four main changes to the macro. It lets the user

- Choose a different source document for the report.
- Choose between transferring only the key data (as before) or all the data.
- Change the title of the document in the dialog box rather than via an input box.
- Decide whether to close the new document or leave it open (for example, so they can inspect it or edit it further).

Add a Userform to the Normal Template

The first step in creating a custom dialog box is to add a userform to the appropriate project—in this case, the Normal template. Here's the easiest way:

1. In the Project Explorer window, right-click Normal and then choose Insert | UserForm from the context menu. The Visual Basic Editor creates a new userform, displays it in a window together with the Toolbox (see Figure 4-2), and gives it the default name, UserForm1.

2. Click the (Name) box at the top of the Properties window, and then type **frmTransfer_Data** as the name for the userform. This is the name by which VBA knows the userform. **frm** is a common prefix for indicating that a name refers to a userform (or "form" for short).

3. Press ENTER to apply the name. You'll see the name in the Forms folder in the Project Explorer change.

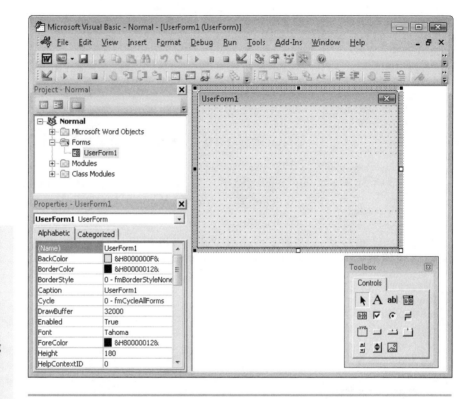

Figure 4-2   Your first move is to add a new userform—essentially a blank sheet—to the Normal template. The userform appears in the Forms folder in the Project Explorer.

MEMO

You can also resize the userform by clicking it and then dragging the handle in the lower-right corner. When you're positioning controls on a userform, having extra space usually helps. When you've got all the controls arranged, you can make the userform smaller so it's not wasting any space.

MEMO

Documents in the Word 2007 .docx format and templates in the Word 2007 .dotx format cannot store VBA code, including userforms.

4. Press DOWN ARROW four times to move the highlight to the Caption property. This property controls the text shown in the title bar of the userform.

5. Type **Transfer Data Macro** as the name for the userform. You'll see the name appear in the title bar of the userform as you type.

6. Press ENTER to apply the change.

7. Move down to the Height property, and increase it to 300 to make the userform substantially taller.

THE EASY WAY

Instead of creating a custom dialog box, you can use one of Word's existing dialog boxes in your actions. For example, if a macro involves the user choosing a document to open, you can summon up Word's Open dialog box. This is not only much easier than creating a custom dialog box with equivalent functionality, but it's also easier for the user, who can open the document in the normal way. Chapter 14 shows you how to use Word's built-in dialog boxes.

52

Add Controls to the Dialog Box

Your next move is to add controls to the dialog box. We'll start by looking at the set of controls that VBA provides, so that you know what raw material is available to you. You'll then place controls on the userform and arrange them so that the form works visually.

Understand the Controls That VBA Provides

VBA provides a set of 14 controls that lets you create custom dialog boxes like those you see in many Windows programs. Table 4-1 explains these controls, and Figure 4-3 shows a custom dialog box that includes the nine most widely useful controls.

You'll be familiar with most of the controls from working in Windows programs. The two controls you may not have used are the tab strip and the toggle button, which have more specialized uses.

MEMO

You can add further controls to the Toolbox as necessary. This topic is beyond the scope of this book.

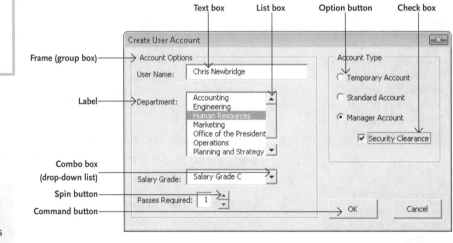

Figure 4-3 This custom dialog box shows the most widely useful controls that VBA offers.

VBA Control Name	English Name	Explanation
Label	Label	Text that appears in the userform. Use for labeling controls such as text boxes or displaying text that the user doesn't need to change.
TextBox	Text box	A box that lets the user enter text or accept a default value.
ListBox	List box	A box that displays a list of existing values so the user can pick one.
ComboBox	Combo box *or* drop-down list	A drop-down list that displays a list of values but also lets the user enter a new value in the text box at the top.
CheckBox	Check box	A check box that lets the user select or clear the box to turn an option on or off.
OptionButton	Option button	A control that lets the user select one of a group of mutually exclusive options.
ToggleButton	Toggle button	A button that lets the user turn an option on or off. The button changes appearance to indicate the change of state.
Frame	Frame *or* group box	A border that you can use to group together other controls to show that they're related.
CommandButton	Command button	A button the user can click to take an action—for example, OK, Cancel, or Print.
TabStrip	Tab strip	A strip of tabs that lets you move from one record to another in a database.
MultiPage	Multipage control *or* "tabs"	A container used to create dialog boxes with different "tabs" containing different controls.
ScrollBar	Scroll bar	A scroll bar for scrolling up and down in a form or another control.
SpinButton	Spin button *or* spinner	A pair of arrow buttons (usually pointing up and down) that the user clicks to adjust the value in a text box. Usually used for numeric values.
Image	Image	A holder for displaying a picture in a dialog box.

Table 4-1   VBA Controls for Creating Custom Dialog Boxes

53

MEMO

Including an image in a dialog box can be visually effective, but you must be sure that the image file is available on the user's computer. If it's not, only the placeholder appears, which spoils the effect.

THE EASY WAY

You can customize the appearance of many controls. For example, for check boxes or option buttons, you can choose between the standard "sunken" look and a "flat" look; or you can place the tabs on a multipage control at the bottom or side instead of the top. For clarity, this book uses the standard appearance for controls.

Many controls have settings that you will need to change frequently. For example, you may find that you

Continued...

Add the Three Frames

To begin, add the three frames to the userform, size them, and align them to each other. Follow these steps:

1.   Click the Frame button in the Toolbox (see Figure 4-4). The mouse pointer changes to a crosshair with a tiny image of a frame next to it.

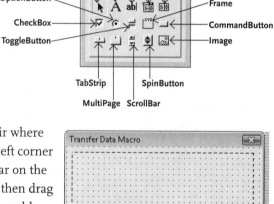

Figure 4-4   To place a control on a userform, click the control's button on the Toolbox, and then click on the userform.

2.   Position the crosshair where you want the upper-left corner of the frame to appear on the userform, click, and then drag to create a frame of roughly the size and shape of that shown on the right here.

3.   With the frame still selected, click in the Properties window and change the following properties to the settings shown:

Property	Setting
(Name)	fraChooseSourceDocument
Caption	1. Choose the Source Document

4. Back in the UserForm window, hold down CTRL while you drag the frame down to below its original position, as shown here. CTRL-dragging like this creates a copy of the object, rather than moving it as a plain drag does. The + sign attached to the mouse pointer indicates that you're making a copy.

5. With the second frame still selected, click in the Properties window and change the following properties to the settings shown:

Property	Setting
(Name)	fraChooseDataToTransfer
Caption	2. Choose the Data to Transfer

6. CTRL-drag the copy of the frame below itself, so that you have three frames of the same size stacked vertically.

7. With the third frame still selected, click in the Properties window and change the following properties to the settings shown:

Property	Setting
(Name)	fraChooseOptions
Caption	3. Choose Options

Add the Labels

Now add the two labels to the form. Follow these steps:

1. Click the Label button in the Toolbox, and then click in the top frame just below the frame's name. The Visual Basic Editor places a standard-size label.

MEMO

If you make a mistake in the Visual Basic Editor, you can usually undo it by pressing CTRL-Z, clicking the Undo button on the Standard toolbar, or choosing Edit | Undo.

2. Click in the Properties window and change the following properties for the label to the settings shown:

Property	Setting
(Name)	lblSourceDocument
Accelerator	S
AutoSize	True
Caption	Source Document:
WordWrap	False

3. CTRL-drag the label down to the third frame to create a copy:

MEMO

The Accelerator property defines the "accelerator key" or "hot key" that the user can press (with Alt) to jump to that control. Because a label is text that you cannot select, pressing the accelerator key for a label causes VBA to select the next control. You may need to change the tab order of the userform to make pressing the accelerator key for the label select the right control. See the end of the chapter for details.

4. With the new label still selected, click in the Properties window and change the following properties for the label to the settings shown:

Property	Setting
(Name)	lblDocumentTitle
Accelerator	T
Caption	Type the Title of the Document:

Add the Combo Box to the Top Frame

Now add the combo box to the top frame. Follow these steps:

1. Click the ComboBox button in the Toolbox, and then click below the Source Document label in the top frame to place a default-size combo box.

2. Drag the right-side handle of the combo box to stretch it out to most of the width of the frame.

3. Click in the Properties window and change the combo box's (Name) property to cmbSourceDocument.

Add the Option Buttons

Next, add the two option buttons to the second frame. Follow these steps:

1. Click the OptionButton button in the Toolbox, and then click in the second frame to place a default-size option button.

2. With the option button still selected, click in the Properties window and change the following properties to the settings shown:

Property	Setting
(Name)	optTransferAllData
Accelerator	A
AutoSize	True
Caption	Transfer All Data
Value	True
WordWrap	False

3. CTRL-drag the option button down to create a second option button below the first.

4. With the second option button still selected, click in the Properties window and set the following properties:

Property	Setting
(Name)	optTransferKeyData
Accelerator	K
Caption	Transfer Only Key Data
Value	False

Add the Text Box and Check Box to the Third Frame

Follow these steps to add the text box and the check box to the third frame:

1. Click the TextBox button on the Toolbox, and then click under the Type the Title of the Document label to place a standard-size text box.

2. Drag the right-side handle on the text box to the right to make the text box almost the full width of the frame.

3. With the text box still selected, click in the Properties window and set the following properties:

Property	Setting
(Name)	txtDocumentTitle
Text	Report Summary

4. Click the CheckBox button on the Toolbox, and then click under the left end of the text box to place a default-size check box.

MEMO

The Value property controls whether the check box is selected (True) or cleared (False). Setting the Value property to True makes VBA select the check box when it displays the dialog box.

5. With the check box still selected, click in the Properties window and set the following properties:

Property	Setting
(Name)	chkCloseNewDocument
Accelerator	C
AutoSize	True
Caption	Close the New Document
Value	True
WordWrap	False

Add the OK Button and Cancel Button

Next, add the OK button and Cancel button to the userform. Follow these steps:

MEMO

Command buttons have a couple of special properties that you're using here. Setting the Default property to True makes the OK command button capture a press of the ENTER key. Similarly, setting the Cancel property to True makes the Cancel command button capture a press of the ESC key. In any dialog box, only one command button can have the Default property set to True, and only one other command button can have the Cancel property set to True.

1. Click the CommandButton item in the Toolbox, and then click in the space near the lower-left corner of the userform to position a standard-size command button.

2. With the command button selected, click in the Properties window and set the following properties:

Property	Setting
(Name)	cmdOK
Accelerator	O
Caption	OK
Default	True
Height	21
Width	55

3. CTRL-drag the command button to the right to create a second command button positioned to the right of the first.

4. With the second command button selected, click in the Properties window and set the following properties:

Property	Setting
(Name)	cmdCancel
Accelerator	C
Cancel	True
Caption	Cancel
Default	False

MEMO

The Visual Basic Editor's snapping feature automatically aligns controls to the nearest grid point, but you will often need to align controls manually to get them laid out precisely.

Align the Controls and Improve the Spacing

To make your userform look tidy and professional, you will probably need to align some of the controls and change the size and spacing of others. This section gives you the general steps for aligning and laying out the controls, leaving you to finesse the specifics. Your goal is to produce a satisfactory and workable arrangement of controls, not necessarily a pixel-perfect clone of the dialog box shown in this chapter.

1. Adjust the third frame to accommodate its contents, and arrange them in it. These are the steps you will typically need to take:

   ▪ Click the frame to select it:

   ▪ Drag the bottom-side handle down to increase the depth of the frame, as shown on the left here.

■ Drag the check box, text box, and (if necessary) the label so that they're comfortably arranged, as shown below.

■ Click the label to select it, and then CTRL-click the text box and check box to add them to the selection, as shown on the left here.

■ Click the one of the selected controls that you want to use as the reference point for the alignment. Here, I'm using the label. The Visual Basic Editor changes the handles around the control to white to indicate that this is the reference point.

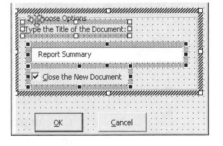

■ Right-click in the selection and choose Align | Lefts from the context menu to align the left points of the other controls with the reference point, as shown on the left here.

■ Choose Format | Vertical Spacing | Make Equal to space the three selected controls out equally within the frame.

2. Follow the same principles as in Step 1 to adjust the contents of the first and second frames as needed.

3. When you've made all three frames suitable sizes, align and arrange the frames themselves:

   ■ Make sure the first frame is positioned suitably in the upper-left corner of the userform. If you're finding it difficult to place the frame where you want it, click it, and then set the Left property (to position the left edge) and the Top property (to position the top) to 6 points.

   ■ Click the second frame, CTRL-click the third frame, and then CTRL-click the first frame. You end up with the three frames selected and the white handles around the first frame.

   ■ Right-click the first frame and choose Align | Lefts to align the second and third frames with the first frame.

   ■ Choose Format | Vertical Spacing | Make Equal to even out the space between the first and second frames and between the second and third frames.

   ■ If there's too much space, choose Format | Vertical Spacing | Decrease; if there's too little space, choose Format | Vertical Spacing | Increase. If the spacing is just right and Goldilocks is happy, do neither.

4. Click one of the command buttons, CTRL-click the other, and then align them, group them, and place them like this:

   ■ Right-click one of the buttons and choose Align | Tops from the context menu to align the tops of the buttons.

   ■ If the buttons are too close together, choose Format | Horizontal Spacing | Increase. If they're too far apart, choose Format | Horizontal Spacing | Decrease. Repeat the command until the buttons are positioned to your satisfaction.

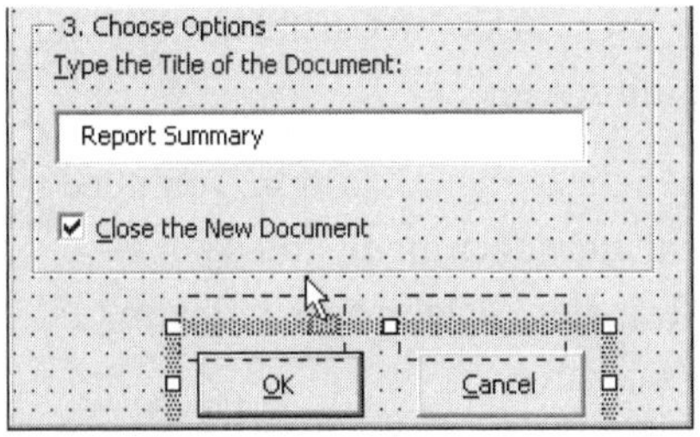

- Right-click one of the buttons and choose Group from the context menu. VBA creates a logical group of the two buttons and puts a box around them.

- Drag the buttons to where you want them to appear in the userform vertically, as shown on the left here.

- Choose Format | Center In Form | Horizontally to make sure the group of buttons is centered horizontally in the userform.

5. If there's extra space at the bottom of the userform, drag the bottom-side handle up to remove all surplus space.

6. Press CTRL-S to save the changes you've made.

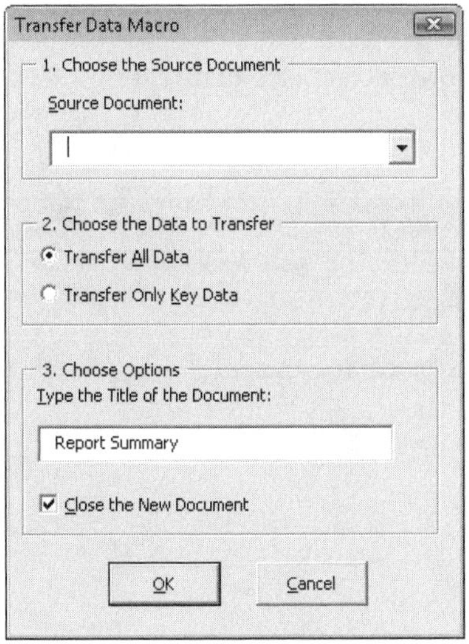

MEMO

When you put controls in a frame, VBA automatically groups them. To move the frame and its contents, simply drag the frame—there's no need to select its contents as well.

So far, you've created the visual aspect of the form—the way it will look when the user displays it. With the userform selected, press F5 or click the Run Sub/UserForm button to display the userform (see Figure 4-5) and the Word window. There's no code hooked up to the userform, but you can check that the controls all look the way they should without the grid you see in the Visual Basic Editor.

Click the Close button (the × button) to close the userform and return to the Visual Basic Editor.

Figure 4-5 Run the userform by pressing F5 to check how it looks. Without code, none of the controls does anything yet.

Add Code to Run the Controls

Now you need to add code that will make the controls work. There are three separate subprocedures:

- **Initializing the userform** You need to add items to the Source Document list box while VBA is loading the userform.

- **Handling the Cancel button**   If the user clicks the Cancel button, you need to remove the userform from the screen.

- **Handling the OK button**   If the user clicks the OK button, you need to open the source document, create the new document, and so on— essentially the same actions in the Transfer_Data macro, but with the trimmings added by the dialog box's controls.

Add the Initialize Procedure for the Userform

Follow these steps to add the Initialize procedure for the userform:

1. From the userform window in the Visual Basic Editor, press F7 to display the Code window for the userform. The Visual Basic Editor automatically creates the stub of a subprocedure for the Click event of the UserForm object (see Figure 4-6).

64

Object drop-down list   Procedure drop-down list

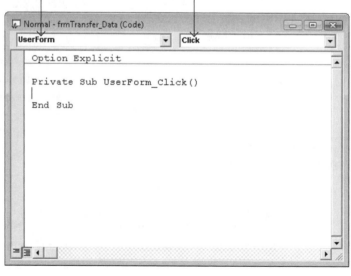

Figure 4-6   The Code window for the userform, with the stub of a UserForm_ Click subprocedure

2. Select the Click part of the stub, and type **Initialize** over it to change the subprocedure to a UserForm_Initialize subprocedure.

3. Move the insertion point to the empty line within the stub.

4. Type **cmb** and press CTRL-SPACEBAR to make AutoComplete enter cmbSourceDocument.

5. Type . (a period) to display the list of properties and methods, type **a** to select the AddItem method, and then press SPACEBAR to enter the AddItem method.

6. Type a space, and then type "**Latest Report.docx**" (including the double quotation marks) as the item you're adding.

7. Add two more items like this:

```
cmbSourceDocument.AddItem "February Report.docx"
cmbSourceDocument.AddItem "March Report.docx"
```

8. Set the Value property of the combo box to "**Latest Document.docx**":

```
cmbSourceDocument.Value ="Latest Report.docx"
```

9. Press F5, and you'll see that the list box is now populated.

10. Click the Close button (the × button) to close the userform again.

WORKING WITH THE ListBox CONTROL

The ListBox control works in almost exactly the same way as the ComboBox control. To populate the list box with the options from which the user can choose, use the AddItem method, as described here for the combo box.

Add the Subprocedure for the OK Button

The subprocedure for the OK button is the most complex part of your custom dialog box. But don't worry—you'll copy most of the code straight across from the Transfer_Data macro.

To create the code for the OK button, follow these steps:

1. On the userform, double-click the OK button. The Visual Basic Editor displays the Code window for the userform and automatically creates the stub of a cmdOK_Click subprocedure:

```
Private Sub cmdOK_Click()

End Sub
```

2. On the blank line, type **Me.Hide**, and then press ENTER.

3. Choose Tools | Macros to open the Macros dialog box.

4. Select the WMME_Transfer_Data_3 macro (the one you edited in Chapter 3).

5. Click the Edit button to open the macro in another Code window.

6. Select all the text from the Documents.Open statement at the beginning to the MsgBox statement at the end.

7. Press CTRL-C (or right-click and choose Copy from the context menu) to copy the code.

8. Click the Close button (the × button) to close the window showing the macro. The Visual Basic Editor puts the focus back in the Code window for the userform.

9. With the insertion point on the blank line in the cmdOK_Click subprocedure, press CTRL-V to paste in the code you copied.

10. Select the pasted code, and then press SHIFT-TAB or click the Outdent button on the Edit toolbar to decrease the indentation. (You may need to indent the beginning of the first line.)

11. Change the Documents.Open statement to read as follows, using the Environ function to return the location of the user's folder, adding \Documents\WMME\ to the path for Windows Vista and \My Documents\WMME\ for Windows XP, and then adding the document name from the combo box:

```
Documents.Open FileName:=Environ("userprofile") & _
    "\Documents\WMME\" & cmbSourceDocument.Value
```

12. Build the two Selection.MoveDown statements into an If... Then... Else condition that checks whether the optTransferKeyData option button's Value property is True. If it is, the macro selects the paragraph as before; if not (meaning that the Transfer All Data option button is selected instead), the macro selects all the content of the document.

```
If optTransferKeyData.Value = True Then
    Selection.MoveDown Unit:=wdParagraph, Count:=1
    Selection.MoveDown Unit:=wdParagraph, _
        Count:=1, Extend:=wdExtend
Else
    ActiveDocument.Content.Select
End If
```

13. Change the ActiveDocument.SaveAs statement to use the Environ function as well, and remove the unnecessary arguments:

```
ActiveDocument.SaveAs FileName:=Environ("userprofile") & _
    "\Documents\WMME\" & "Report Summary.docx" _
    FileFormat:=wdFormatXMLDocument
```

14. Move down to the Selection:TypeText Text:=InputBox statement, and change it to "type" the text from the Document Title text box instead:

```
Selection.TypeText Text:=txtDocumentTitle.Text
```

15. Go to the ActiveDocument.Close statement at the end of the macro and put it in an If statement that checks whether the Close the New Document check box is selected:

```
If chkCloseNewDocument.Value = True Then
    ActiveDocument.Close
End If
```

16. Finally, type the **Unload Me** command at the end of the subprocedure to remove the userform from memory.

Here's the full code listing that you should have now:

```
Private Sub cmdok_click()
    Me.Hide
    Documents.Open FileName:=Environ("userprofile") & _
        "\Documents\WMME\" & cmbSourceDocument.Value
    If optTransferKeyData.Value = True Then
        Selection.MoveDown Unit:=wdParagraph, Count:=1
        Selection.MoveDown Unit:=wdParagraph, _
            Count:=1, Extend:=wdExtend
    Else
        ActiveDocument.Content.Select
    End If
    Selection.Copy
    ActiveDocument.Close
    Documents.Add DocumentType:=wdNewBlankDocument
    Selection.Style = ActiveDocument.Styles("Heading 1")
    Selection.TypeText Text:=txtDocumentTitle.Text
    Selection.TypeParagraph
    Selection.TypeText _
        Text:="Here is the latest report summary:"
    Selection.TypeParagraph
    Selection.PasteAndFormat (wdPasteDefault)
    ActiveDocument.SaveAs FileName:= _
        Environ("userprofile") & "\Documents\WMME\" _
        & "Report Summary.docx", FileFormat:= _
        wdFormatXMLDocument
```

```
        If chkCloseNewDocument.Value = True Then
            ActiveDocument.Close
        End If
        MsgBox "The macro has created the report summary.", _
            vbOKOnly + vbInformation, "Transfer Data Macro"
        Unload Me
    End Sub
```

Add the Subprocedure for the Cancel Button

Now, add the subprocedure for the Cancel button. Follow these steps:

1. In the Code window, click after the end of the cmdOK_Click subprocedure.

2. Click the Object drop-down list in the upper-left corner of the Code window, and then choose cmdCancel from the list:

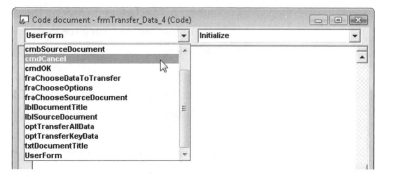

3. The Visual Basic Editor automatically inserts the stub of a Click event procedure for the cmdCancel button:

```
Private Sub cmdCancel_Click()

End Sub
```

4. Type two lines of code inside the stub, as shown here:

```
Private Sub cmdCancel_Click()
    Me.Hide
    Unload Me
End Sub
```

5. Press CTRL-S or click the Save button on the Standard toolbar to save your work.

Test the Dialog Box

You're ready to test whether the dialog box works. Try testing in two ways:

- First, click in the Code window in one of the subprocedures (it doesn't matter which), and press F8 to start running the code one statement at a time. You'll see VBA work through the UserForm_Initialize subprocedure before displaying the dialog box. And when you click one of the buttons, you'll see that code too execute statement by statement.

- Second, click the userform itself, and press F5 to run the code at full speed. The dialog box opens immediately—and when you click one of the buttons, the code executes quickly.

Create a Way of Displaying the Dialog Box

Finally, you need to create a macro that will launch the dialog box from Word rather than from the Visual Basic Editor. You can do this in moments:

1. Right-click the Normal item in the Project Explorer and choose Insert | Module from the context menu to insert a new module. The Visual Basic Editor opens a Code window for the module.

2. Press F4 to put the focus in the Properties window.

CHECK AND CHANGE THE TAB ORDER OF THE DIALOG BOX

If you test all the accelerator keys in the dialog box, you'll find that pressing ALT-T to reach the Document Title text box actually selects the Close The New Document check box instead. This is because the text box isn't immediately after its label in the *tab order* of the userform.

To change the tab order, click the third frame, and then choose View | Tab Order to open the Tab Order dialog box for the frame (shown here). Use the Move Up button and Move Down button to shuffle the controls into the right order: lblDocumentTitle, txtDocumentTitle, and then chkCloseNewDocument.

Test the dialog box again and see the effect of the change.

Press TAB to move through the controls in the dialog box. Note any other changes you need to make, and then use the Tab Order dialog box to make them. There's a tab order for the dialog box as a whole and a separate one for each frame.

71

3. Type **WMME_Chapter_4** as the name for the module.

4. Click in the Code window and type the following short macro:

```
Sub WMME_Run_Transfer_Data_Macro()
    frmTransfer_Data.Show
End Sub
```

5. Press CTRL-S or click the Save button on the Standard toolbar to save your work.

You can now run this macro from the Macros dialog box in Word, or create a Quick Access Toolbar button or keyboard shortcut for it as you learned to do in Chapter 1.

Repeat Actions with Loops

To produce the documents you want by using macros, you'll often need to repeat actions. For example, you may need to create several new documents, or take the same action for each paragraph in a document that's formatted with the Normal style. This chapter shows you how to repeat actions however many times you need, whether it be a set number of times or a number of times decided by the contents of the documents or the choice of the user who runs the macro.

Understand VBA's Different Ways of Repeating Actions

The simplest way to repeat an action in VBA is to repeat the command for the action. This is called *hard-coding* and works well for simple tasks.

For example, if you need to create two new documents using the Normal template, as you've done in the macro you recorded and edited, you can simply repeat the Documents.Add command like this:

```
Documents.Add
Documents.Add
```

UNDERSTAND THE TECHNICAL TERMS FOR LOOPS

Here are the terms you need to know when working with loops:

■ **Iteration** Running through the loop one time.

■ **Fixed-iteration loop** A loop that runs a set number of times.

■ **Indefinite loop** A loop that runs a flexible number of times (depending on conditions).

■ **Loop invariant** The expression that determines whether the loop runs. For example, if you have a loop for going to the gym, you may have a loop invariant that says "If it's Monday, Wednesday, or Friday, go to the gym."

MEMO

Loops make your code easier to test and easier to debug.

This works fine—and *is* fine—even if it makes professional programmers sniff in disgust. But if you need to make your code flexible—so that it can create different numbers of documents as needed, or work through every paragraph in a document—you can use loops to repeat actions instead.

As its name suggests, a *loop* is a section of code that VBA can go around and repeat rather than simply going through. If the conditions are right, VBA repeats the loop; otherwise, it goes on to the next section of code.

Get an Overview of the Types of Loops That VBA Offers

VBA offers several different kinds of loops, but some of them are specialized and seldom used. This chapter shows you how to use the three most useful kinds of loop:

■ **For... Next loop** Lets you repeat an action a set number of times. You can hard-code the number of times or let the user choose it by using an input box or dialog box.

■ **For Each... Next loop** Lets you repeat an action once for each object in a VBA collection. For example, you can repeat an action once for each of the paragraphs in a document. Flexible and useful.

- **Do While … Loop loop**   Lets you repeat an action as long as a condition is true. The loop checks whether the condition is true, runs if it is, and then checks again.

Get Set Up to Work Through This Chapter

Before you start working with loops, open the Visual Basic Editor and create a new module in which you can create the macros. Follow these steps:

1. Open Microsoft Word if it's not already running.

2. Click the Developer tab, go to the Code group, and then click Visual Basic to open the Visual Basic Editor.

3. If the Visual Basic Editor opens a Code window for a module you worked with recently, click the window's Close button (the × button) to close it.

4. Right-click the Normal template and then choose Insert | Module from the context menu to insert a new module in the Normal template.

5. Press F4 to put the focus in the Properties window.

6. Type **WMME_Chapter_5** as the new name for the module, replacing the default name (such as Module1), and press ENTER to apply the change.

Okay, you're ready to start creating loops.

Repeat an Action a Set Number of Times

When you need to repeat an action a set number of times, use a For … Next loop.

In a For... Next loop, you don't have to specify the *counter* variable after the Next keyword—that's why *counter* is in brackets in the syntax after Next. But having *counter* there helps keep your code clear when you have multiple loops, and it's easy to add, so there's no downside.

Understand How the For... Next Loop Works

The For... Next loop looks like this:

```
For counter = start to end [Step stepsize]
      [take actions here]
[Exit For]
      [take more actions here]
Next [counter]
```

The loop starts with the For keyword and the *counter* variable and ends with the Next keyword. Normally, you specify the *counter* variable after the Next keyword to make clear which loop is ending.

counter is a numeric variable that controls how the loop runs. *start* is the starting value of *counter*, and *end* is the ending value. For example, the following statement uses a variable called intCounter to make the loop run five times, from intCounter = 1 to intCounter = 5:

```
For intCounter = 1 to 5
```

Exit For is an optional statement for exiting a For loop before the loop has finished executing. For example, your code may run into a situation where

MOVING THROUGH THE LOOP IN LARGER STEPS

Normally, VBA increases the value of *counter* by 1 on each iteration of the loop, as in the previous example. But you can use the optional Step keyword with the *stepsize* variable or expression to either increase the value of *counter* by larger steps or decrease it (either by 1 each iteration or by a larger amount).

For example, the following statement uses the Step keyword with a *stepsize* of 10, so the loop runs ten times:

```
For intCounter = 0 To 100 Step 10
```

The following statement uses a negative *stepsize* to reduce intCounter from 10 to 0, so the loop runs five times:

```
For intCounter = 10 to 0 Step -2
```

you don't want to take the remaining actions in the loop—so instead, you can use an Exit For statement to leave the loop at the appropriate point.

Put For... Next Loops into Action

This section contains two examples of For... Next loops. The first uses a hard-coded loop, while the second lets the user control the loop via an input box.

Using a Hard-Coded For... Next Loop

First, try this example of a For... Next loop that creates five new documents:

1. Click in the Code sheet for the WMME_Chapter_5 module.

2. Type the Sub declaration for the macro:

   ```
   Sub WMME_For_Next_Loop_1
   ```

3. Press ENTER to make the Visual Basic Editor add the parentheses and the End Sub statement to the stub:

   ```
   Sub WMME_For_Next_Loop_1()

   End Sub
   ```

4. With the insertion point on the blank line within the stub, type the following lines of code:

   ```
   Dim intCounter As Integer
   For intCounter = 1 to 5
       Documents.Add
   Next intCounter
   ```

Here's the complete macro:

```
Sub WMME_For_Next_Loop_1()
    Dim intCounter As Integer
    For intCounter = 1 to 5
        Documents.Add
    Next intCounter
End Sub
```

MEMO

Use the Visual Basic Editor code-completion features that you learned how to use earlier in this book. For example, once you've declared the Integer variable intCounter, you can enter it quickly by typing **intc** and then pressing CTRL-SPACEBAR.

Here's what happens in the macro:

- The Dim intCounter As Integer statement declares a variable named intCounter as being of the Integer type. (That means the variable can contain only whole numbers, not fractions.)

- VBA assigns the intCounter variable the value 1.

- VBA performs the Documents.Add command, creating a new document based on the Normal template.

- VBA evaluates the Next intCounter statement. Because intCounter's value is less than the ending value (5), VBA increases the value of intCounter by 1, and then runs the loop again, repeating it until intCounter's value is 5.

Click in the macro and press F5 (or click the Run Sub/UserForm button) to run it. You'll see five new Word documents spring into existence.

Leave these documents open—you'll close them a little later in this chapter.

Using an Input Box to Control a For... Next Loop

Now try this example that uses an input box to let the user decide how many documents to create:

1. In the WMME_Chapter_5 module, select the WMME_For_Next_Loop_1 macro you just created.

2. Right-click the selection and then choose Copy from the context menu to copy the macro to the Clipboard.

3. Right-click below the macro in the Code sheet and then choose Paste to paste in the macro.

4. Edit the macro to read like this:

```
Sub WMME_For_Next_Loop_2()
    Dim intCounter As Integer
    Dim intEnd As Integer
```

```
        intEnd = InputBox _
            ("Type the number of documents to create:", _
            "Create New Documents", "3")
        For intCounter = 1 to intEnd
            Documents.Add
        Next intCounter
    End Sub
```

This example works in the same way as the previous example, except for the following:

■ Dim intEnd As Integer creates an Integer variable named intEnd.

■ The intEnd = InputBox statement displays an input box (as shown here) prompting the user to decide how many new documents to create. The default value is 3. When the user enters the number and clicks the OK button (or presses ENTER), VBA assigns the value to the intEnd variable.

■ The For intCounter = 1 to IntEnd statement runs from intCounter = 1 to intCounter = intEnd, creating a document at each iteration until it reaches the number the user entered.

Try running this macro by clicking in it and then pressing F5 or clicking the Run Sub/UserForm button. Up comes the input box, and when you enter a number and then click OK, Word creates that number of documents.

Again, leave the documents open. We'll deal with them next.

Repeat an Action for Each Object in a Collection

Often in your macros, you'll need to repeat an action for each object in a collection—but you won't know how many objects there are. Now, you can find out the number of items in a collection by getting the Count property, and then use a For... Next loop to go through each of them. But what's easier is to use a For Each... Next loop, which is specially designed for looping through each item in a collection.

In this section, you'll use a For Each... Next loop to close each open document, saving any unsaved changes if you want to. First, though, a dash of theory.

Understand How the For Each... Next Loop Works

The For Each... Next loop looks like this:

```
For Each object In collection
     [statements]
[Exit For]
     [statements]
Next [object]
```

The For Each... Next loop works in a very similar way to the For... Next loop, except that it's driven by the collection you specify rather than by a variable. VBA counts the number of items in the collection, and then (assuming there's at least one object) performs the statements specified in the loop on the object.

As with the For... Next loop, you can exit early from the For Each... Next loop by using an Exit For statement. For example, you can use a For Each... Next loop to go through the objects in a collection until you find the object you're interested in. You can then take whatever actions you need on that object and exit the loop rather than plowing through the remaining objects in the collection.

If you've still got a couple of handfuls of new documents open from the previous two examples, you're all set. Otherwise, simply press CTRL-N in Word a few times to create some new documents that you can close.

Put For Each... Next Loops into Action

Try this example of a For... Next loop so that you can see how it works.
Follow these steps:

1. Click below the second macro in the WMME_Chapter_5 Code sheet, and then type the Sub statement for a new macro:

```
Sub WMME_For_Each_Next_Loop
```

2. Press ENTER to make the Visual Basic Editor add the parentheses and the End Sub statement to the stub:

```
Sub WMME_For_Each_Next_Loop()

End Sub
```

3. With the insertion point on the blank line within the stub, type the following lines of code:

```
Dim myDocument As Document
For Each myDocument In Documents
    myDocument.Close SaveChanges:=wdPromptToSaveChanges
Next myDocument
```

Here's the complete macro:

```
Sub WMME_For_Each_Next_Loop()
    Dim myDocument As Document
    For Each myDocument In Documents
        myDocument.Close SaveChanges:=wdPromptToSaveChanges
    Next myDocument
End Sub
```

Here's what happens in this macro:

- The Dim myDocument As Document statement declares an object variable named myDocument that is of the Document type.

MEMO

If a document is "clean," meaning it contains no un-saved changes, the myDocument.Close statement simply closes it. A new docu-ment in which you've made no changes is considered clean. As soon as you type a character or make another change in it, it becomes "dirty."

- The For Each... Next loop runs once for each myDocument object in the Documents collection—in other words, once for each open document. The myDocument.Close statement closes each myDocument object in turn, prompting the user to save changes.

Step through the code by pressing F8, or run it by pressing F5 or clicking the Run Sub/UserForm button. Word closes each open document in turn, prompting you to save any that contain unsaved changes:

TRY USING AN EXIT FOR STATEMENT TO QUIT A FOR LOOP

Sometimes you'll need to quit a For loop without completing an iteration or without reaching the limit set by the loop invariant. To quit the loop, use an Exit For statement like this:

```
Sub WWME_For_Next_Loop_Using_Exit_For()
    Dim myWindow As Window
    For Each myWindow In Windows
        myWindow.Close
        If MsgBox("Do you want to
continue closing windows?", _
            vbYesNo + vbQuestion, "Close
Open Windows") = _
            vbNo Then Exit For
    Next myWindow
End Sub
```

This macro declares a variable called myWindow as being a Window object, then uses myWindow to loop through the Windows collection, which contains a Window object for each open window. As you probably know, you can open multiple windows on

the same document, which is often useful for looking at different parts of the document at the same time or using different views (for example, Draft view and Outline view) in different windows.

The macro first closes a window, and then displays a message box (shown here) prompting the user to decide whether to continue closing windows. If the user clicks the No button, the Exit For statement exits the For loop.

To try out this macro, press CTRL-N to open a new document, and then choose View | Window | New Window one or more times to open extra windows. Press F8 to step through the macro, and watch the result.

82

Repeat an Action if a Condition Is True

At other times, you may need to repeat an action based on a condition—either until the condition is met or until it becomes false. VBA lets you do this in several different ways. We'll look at the most useful way here: the Do While... Loop loop, which lets you repeat an action as long as the condition remains true.

Understand How the Do While... Loop Loop Works

The Do While... Loop loop looks like this:

```
Do While condition
    [statements]
[Exit Do]
    [statements]
Loop
```

Here's what happens:

- At the Do While statement, VBA checks whether the condition is true. If it is, VBA executes the statements in the loop, arrives at the Loop statement ending the loop, and then goes back to the beginning.

- If the condition isn't true, VBA skips straight to the statement after the Loop statement.

- If you need to exit early from the loop without completing an iteration, you can position an Exit Do statement at any point within it. Usually, you'd use a condition with the Exit Do statement to prevent VBA from exiting the loop during a normal iteration.

Put Do While... Loop Loops into Action

Try this example of a Do While... Loop loop:

1. Run the WMME_For_Next_Loop_2 macro you created earlier in the chapter, and have it create a handful of documents.

2. Click in empty space at the bottom of the Code sheet, and then enter this short macro:

```
Sub WMME_Do_While_Loop_Loop()
    Do While Documents.Count > 1
        Documents(1).Close SaveChanges:=wdSaveChanges
    Loop
End Sub
```

Here's what happens in this macro:

- The Do While statement evaluates the condition Documents.Count > 1—whether the Count property of the Documents collection is greater than 1. If so, more than one document is open, and the loop runs.

- The Documents(1).Close SaveChanges:=wdSaveChanges statement closes the first document in the Documents collection, saving any unsaved changes it contains. After the first document closes, the second document becomes the new first document, and so on.

- The Loop statement sends execution back up to the Do While statement, where the loop repeats.

Try running the macro by clicking in it and pressing F5 or clicking the Run Sub/UserForm button. Word closes all documents except for one.

UNDERSTAND VBA'S FOUR KINDS OF DO LOOPS

VBA provides four different kinds of Do loops, but this chapter discusses in detail only the most useful kind, the Do While… Loop loop.

Here are brief details on the other three kinds of Do loops in case you run into them in other people's code or you want to investigate them yourself:

- A Do… Loop While loop performs its actions once, and then tests the condition to see whether it should run again. It runs again if the condition is true. Usually, it's easier to use the Do… Loop Until loop, which runs again until the condition becomes true, continuing to loop while the condition remains false.

- A Do… Loop Until loop performs actions once, and then tests the condition to see whether it should run again. It runs again if the condition is false.

- A Do Until… Loop loop evaluates its condition and runs if it is false, continuing to run until the condition becomes true. Most people find it easier to use a Do While… Loop loop, which evaluates its condition and runs if it is true, continuing to run until the condition becomes false.

Make Decisions in Your Macros

In some macros, you'll always need to take the same actions—for example, creating a new document, entering some boilerplate text in it, and applying formatting. But more often, you'll need to make decisions in your macros and take action accordingly. This chapter shows you how to make decisions, building on what you've learned informally about decision making in VBA in the earlier chapters.

Understand the Decision-Making Tools VBA Gives You

VBA gives you two main tools for making decisions:

- **If statements**   These statements are for deciding among two or more situations. VBA lets you use several different types of If statements, all of which you'll meet in this chapter.

- **Select Case statements**   These statements simplify deciding among many situations. VBA provides only one type of Select Case statement.

Get Set Up to Work Through This Chapter

Before you start working with decisions, follow these steps to open the Visual Basic Editor and create a new module in which you can create the macros:

1. Open Microsoft Word if it's not already running.

2. Click the Developer tab, go to the Code group, and then click Visual Basic to open the Visual Basic Editor.

3. If the Visual Basic Editor opens a Code window for a module you worked with recently, click the window's Close button (the × button) to close it.

4. Right-click the Normal template and then choose Insert | Module from the context menu to insert a new module in the Normal template.

5. Press F4 to put the focus in the Properties window.

6. Type **WMME_Chapter_6** as the new name for the module, replacing the default name (such as Module1), and press ENTER to apply the change.

You're now ready to start working with If statements.

Use If Statements in Your Macros

If statements provide an easy way to make decisions in your code. In fact, they're so essential to programming in VBA that you've already seen some If statements earlier in this book.

VBA provides three kinds of If statements:

- **If… Then**   For checking a single condition and taking an action if it is met

- **If... Then... Else**   For checking a single condition, taking an action it it's met, and taking a different action if it's not met

- **If... Then... ElseIf... Else**   For checking two or more conditions, taking the appropriate action if a condition is met, and optionally taking a different action if no condition is met

Check One Condition with an If... Then Statement

To check a single condition, use an If... Then statement. You normally write it as a block of code like this, starting with the If statement and its condition and ending with the End If statement:

```
If condition Then
    statements
End If
```

Here, *condition* is the condition you want to check. If the condition is true, VBA runs the statements within the block. If not, VBA skips to the End If line, and then continues running any statements after it in the macro.

Here's an example of an If... Then statement you met in Chapter 3:

```
If MsgBox("Create a new document?", vbYesNo + vbQuestion, _
    "Create New Document") = vbYes Then
    Documents.Add
End If
```

If the user clicks the Yes button in the message box, the message box returns the constant vbYes, and the Documents.Add statement on the next line creates a new document. If the user clicks the No button, VBA goes on to the next statement after the End If line.

Decide Among Two Courses of Action with an If... Then... Else Statement

Often, you'll need to decide between two paths in your code: if a condition is true, do this; if it's not true, do something else instead.

MEMO

You can also use a single-line If statement that reads **If** *condition* **Then** *statement*—for example, If intNumber = 1 Then MsgBox "intNumber is 1." This type of If statement is more compact and has no End If line; you've seen an example earlier in this book. However, laying your code out in block If statements makes it easier to read and to debug, so it's usually a better idea.

In VBA, you use an If... Then... Else statement to make this kind of decision:

```
If condition Then
    [statements]
Else
    [statements]
End If
```

If the condition is true, VBA runs the statements before the Else keyword. If the condition is False, VBA runs the statements after the Else keyword.

Follow these steps to create an example of an If... Then... Else statement:

1. Click below the Option Explicit line in your new WMME_Chapter_6 Code sheet, and then type the macro's name:

```
Sub WMME_If_Then_Condition
```

2. Press ENTER to have the Visual Basic Editor create the rest of the stub for you:

```
Sub WMME_If_Then_Condition()

End Sub
```

3. Inside the stub, declare a String variable named strUserName to hold the username the user types:

```
Dim strUserName As String
```

4. Below that, declare a String variable called strTitle to hold the title of the message box and input box the macro will display, and then assign the text "User Name Macro" to the variable:

```
Dim strTitle As String
strTitle = "User Name Macro"
```

5. On the next line, type a label named **GetUserName:** (including the colon, which tells VBA it's a label):

```
GetUserName:
```

MEMO

A *label* is a named point in the code to which you can go using a GoTo statement. You'll notice that when you type the colon after the label's name and press ENTER or move to a new line, VBA automatically removes any indent from the label line, making the label begin flush with the Sub statement.

6. Add an input box that assigns what the user enters to the strUserName String variable. The input box has the prompt "Enter your name:" and displays the contents of the strTitle String variable in its title bar:

```
strUserName = InputBox("Enter your name:", strTitle)
```

7. Type the If condition as shown next. If the strUserName string is blank (because the user has clicked the Cancel button or clicked the OK button without typing text in the input box), the GoTo statement sends the macro back to the GetUserName label, making the input box appear again until the user enters a usable name. Otherwise, the Else statement displays a message box showing the name the user typed.

```
If strUserName = "" Then
    GoTo GetUserName
Else
    MsgBox "Your name is " & strUserName & ".", _
        vbOKOnly + vbInformation, strTitle
End If
```

Here's what the whole macro looks like:

```
Sub WMME_If_Then_Else_Condition()
    Dim strUserName As String
    Dim strTitle As String
    strTitle = "User Name Macro"
GetUserName:
    strUserName = InputBox("Enter your name:", strTitle)
    If strUserName = "" Then
        GoTo GetUserName
    Else
        MsgBox "Your name is " & strUserName & ".", _
            vbOKOnly + vbInformation, strTitle
    End If
End Sub
```

Try stepping through the macro by clicking in it and pressing F8 to execute one statement at a time. The first time the input box appears, click its Cancel button to test the GoTo statement. When the input box reappears, leave the text box blank, and click the OK button. The third time the input box appears, type a name and click OK. Verify that the name appears in the message box.

Choose Among Multiple Courses of Action with an If... Then... ElseIf... Else Statement

When you need to choose among three or more courses of action in a macro, you can use either an If... Then... ElseIf... Else... statement (discussed in this section) or a Select Case statement (discussed in the next section).

Here's how an If... Then... ElseIf... Else... statement looks:

```
If condition1 Then
    statements1
ElseIf condition2 Then
    statements2
[other ElseIf statements here as needed]
Else
    statements
End If
```

As you can see, this works in the same way as the If... Then... Else statement except that it also has one or more ElseIf statements between the If line and the Else line.

Take the following steps to create a macro containing an If... Then... Else statement. The macro displays an input box prompting the user to enter their birth year, then displays a message box telling the user whether they are too young for whatever the macro does (I'll leave this to your imagination), too old, or just right.

1. Click in open space in the WMME_Chapter_6 Code sheet, and then type the macro's name:

   ```
   Sub WMME_If_Then_Else_Condition
   ```

2. Press ENTER to have the Visual Basic Editor create the rest of the stub for you:

```
Sub WMME_If_Then_Else_Condition()

End Sub
```

3. Inside the stub, declare an Integer variable called intYear to hold the year the user types, and then assign to it the result of an input box that prompts the user to type their birth year:

```
Dim intYear As Integer
intYear = InputBox("Type your birth year:", "Birth Year")
```

4. Type the If... Then... ElseIf... Else statement as follows. After you've created the first MsgBox line, use Copy and Paste (or CTRL-drag-and-drop, if you prefer) to create the subsequent MsgBox lines quickly rather than typing each of them.

```
If intYear > 1995 Then
    MsgBox "You are too young.", vbOKOnly + _
        vbInformation, "Age Check"
ElseIf intYear < 1900 Then
    MsgBox "You are too old.", vbOKOnly + _
        vbInformation, "Age Check"
Else
    MsgBox "You are the right age.", vbOKOnly + _
        vbInformation, "Age Check"
End If
```

Here's the whole macro:

```
Sub WMME_If_Then_Else_Condition()
    Dim intYear As Integer
    intYear = InputBox("Type your birth year:", "Birth Year")
    If intYear > 1995 Then
        MsgBox "You are too young.", vbOKOnly + _
            vbInformation, "Age Check"
```

MEMO

You can use as many ElseIf statements as you want. But if you find yourself using more than a handful, consider using a Select Case statement instead. See the next section for details on the Select Case statement.

```
    ElseIf intYear < 1900 Then
        MsgBox "You are too old.", vbOKOnly + _
            vbInformation, "Age Check"
    Else
        MsgBox "You are the right age.", vbOKOnly + _
            vbInformation, "Age Check"
    End IfEnd Sub
```

Run the macro by clicking in it and pressing F5 or clicking the Run Sub/ UserForm button. Type a birth year between 1900 and 1995 to produce the message box telling you that you're the right age.

Run the macro twice more. The first time, give a birth year before 1900. The second time, give a birth year after 1995. Watch the message boxes you get.

Use Select Case Statements

When you need to find which of many possible situations is true, use a Select Case statement rather than an extended If... Then... ElseIf statement.

A Select Case statement is a more compact way of testing multiple conditions, and in theory will make your code run faster. In practice, you probably won't notice the difference, but a Select Case statement is also quicker to code and easier to debug than a long If statement, so it's a handy tool to have in your kit.

Understand How the Select Case Statement Works

The Select Case statement looks like this:

```
Select Case TestExpression
    Case Expression1
        [Statements1]
    Case Expression2
        [Statements2]
```

MEMO

The macro doesn't check that the date is a valid integer, so you can cause an error by entering text rather than a number. You can also cause an error by entering an integer that's too large for the Integer data type (which goes up to 32,767). More on this in the next chapter—but try entering 33333 or a higher number if you'd like a quick taste of a VBA error.

```
    [Case Else]
        [StatementsElse]
End Select
```

Don't worry if that looks a bit daunting: you'll get the hang of it in a moment. Here's what happens:

- The Select Case keywords start the Select Case statement, and the End Select keywords end the statement.

- *TestExpression* is the expression with which you're comparing the other expressions. For example, Select Case ActiveDocument.Words.Count performs the comparison with the number of words in the active document.

- The various Case *Expression* lines give the expressions with which VBA compares *TestExpression*. For example, Case *Expression1* is the first comparison, and the statements after it are those that run if the test expression matches the first expression. So if you have Case Is < 20 as the first test expression, and the active document contains 20 or fewer words, *Statements1* will run.

- The optional Case Else line lets you run statements (*StatementsElse*) if the test expression matches none of the cases you define.

Put a Select Case Statement into Action

To try a Select Case statement, create the macro described here. The macro works with the word count in the active document. Follow these steps:

THE EASY WAY

If you need to add more words to your document quickly, press F4 to repeat the last text you typed.

1. Make sure you have a document open in Word. Type a few words in it—as many as you like.

2. In the Code sheet for the WMME_Chapter_6 module, click in open space below the last macro, and then type the macro's name:

```
Sub WMME_Select_Case
```

3. Press ENTER to have the Visual Basic Editor create the rest of the stub for you:

```
Sub WMME_Select Case()

End Sub
```

4. Inside the stub, declare a String variable called strMessage to contain the text for the message box the macro will display:

```
Dim strMessage As String
```

5. Start the Select Case statement like this, using the test expression ActiveDocument.Words.Count (which returns the number of words in the active document):

```
Select Case ActiveDocument.Words.Count
```

6. Add the first Case statement like this, assigning text to the strMessage variable if the word count is 1:

```
Case Is = 1
    strMessage = "The document contains no words at all."
```

7. Copy the first Case statement and paste it four times, then modify the pasted sections so that you have this:

```
Case Is = 1
    strMessage = "The document contains no words at all."
Case Is < 20
    strMessage = "The document contains fewer than 20 words."
Case Is < 50
    strMessage = "The document contains fewer than 50 words."
Case Is < 100
    strMessage = "The document contains fewer than 100 words."
Case Else
    strMessage = "The document contains more than 100 words."
```

MEMO

Even when a document is empty, the Count property of its Words collection returns 1 rather than 0. (Don't ask.)

8.   Add the End Select statement and an OK-only message box displaying the strMessage variable:

```
End Select
MsgBox strMessage, vbOKOnly + vbInformation, _
    "Select Case Example"
```

Here's the complete macro:

```
Sub WMME_Select_Case()
    Dim strMessage As String
    Select Case ActiveDocument.Words.Count
    Case Is = 1
        strMessage = "The document contains no words at all."
    Case Is < 20
        strMessage = "The document contains fewer than 20 words."
    Case Is < 50
        strMessage = "The document contains fewer than 50 words."
    Case Is < 100
        strMessage = "The document contains fewer than 100 words."
    Case Else
        strMessage = "The document contains more than 100 words."
    End Select
    MsgBox strMessage, vbOKOnly + vbInformation, _
        "Select Case Example"
End Sub
```

Test the macro by clicking in it and pressing F5 or clicking the Run Sub/ UserForm button. Change the number of words in your document and run it again, making sure each of the Case statements works.

Use Variables and Constants

Often, you'll need to store data temporarily in your macros so that you can use it later. To do so, you use variables. For example, instead of asking the user to input their name at each point you need it in the macro, you can ask for the user's name one time via an input box, store the result in a variable, and then insert that variable throughout the macro.

In this chapter, you'll learn how to declare variables and how to use them in your code. You'll also learn how to declare and use constants, which are set values that you can use easily throughout your macros.

Get Set Up to Work Through This Chapter

To give yourself space to work with variables and constants, follow these steps to open the Visual Basic Editor and create a new module in which you can create the macros:

1. Open Microsoft Word if it's not already running.

2. Click the Developer tab, go to the Code group, and then click Visual Basic to open the Visual Basic Editor.

3. If the Visual Basic Editor opens a Code window for a module you worked with recently, click the window's Close button (the × button) to close it.

4. Right-click the Normal template and then choose Insert | Module from the context menu to insert a new module in the Normal template.

5. Press F4 to put the focus in the Properties window.

6. Type **WMME_Chapter_7** as the new name for the module, replacing the default name (such as Module1), and press ENTER to apply the change.

7. Repeat steps 4 through 6 to create a new module named **WMME_Chapter_7_2**.

You're now ready to start working through this chapter.

Use Variables in Your Macros

A variable is a named area in memory in which you can store data. For example, in Chapter 5, you used a variable named intCounter to store an integer value that increased as the loop ran.

Declare a Variable

To create a variable, you *declare* it. Declaring simply means telling VBA that you want to use the variable name you give and (optionally) telling VBA the type of data the variable will hold.

VBA lets you declare variables in two ways: *explicitly* and *implicitly*.

Declare a Variable Explicitly

Declaring a variable explicitly means that you tell VBA about the variable before you start using it. This is the best way of using variables, because it lets VBA alert you to several errors that can creep in with implicit declarations.

LEARN THE RULES FOR NAMING YOUR VARIABLES

You can create many different types of variable names to make your variables easy to recognize.

VBA puts the following rules on the characters you can use to create names:

- Each variable name must start with a letter. You can't start a name with a number or a symbol.

- Each name can be up to 255 characters long. Shorter is usually better.

- You can use letters, numbers, and underscores but no spaces.

- You can't use periods, exclamation points, mathematical operators (such as + and –), or comparison operators (such as =, <, >, or <=).

- You can use the type-declaration characters (@, &, $, and #) only at the end of variables to declare their types. You can't use these characters within the names. Generally, it's easiest to avoid using these characters.

Apart from these rules about characters, there are two rules about the names themselves:

- Each variable name has to be unique within the area of VBA in which you're using it. This is simply so that VBA can be sure which variable you're telling it to use. The areas of VBA are called "scopes," and you'll learn about them later in this chapter.

- You're not supposed to use any of the names that VBA uses. For example, since Word VBA uses a Document object, you shouldn't create a variable named Document. Doing so causes confusion, because you then have to tell VBA whether you mean your Document variable or its own Document object.

Beyond these restrictions, it's a good idea to name your variables clearly and consistently. Table 7-1 (later in this chapter) shows suggested three-letter prefixes that you can use to make clear what data type each variable has—for example, in this scheme the int prefix on a variable named intCounter indicates that the variable has the Integer data type.

To declare a variable explicitly, you use the appropriate one of four keywords: Dim, Private, Public, or Static. The keywords create different types of variables, as you'll see in a minute. For now, try this quick example:

1. Click in the Code window for the WMME_Chapter_7 module.

2. Type the following macro, using the skills you've learned in the previous chapters:

```
Sub WMME_Variables_1()
    Dim strText As String
    strText = "Hi! How are you?"
    MsgBox strText
End Sub
```

3. Click in the macro, and then press F8 to step through it. You'll see this.

You can easily grasp what happens:

- The Dim statement declares a variable named strText as being of the String data type. (More on this shortly.)

- The next line assigns a string of text ("Hi! How are you?") to the variable.

- The MsgBox line displays a message box containing the variable's contents.

Declare a Variable Implicitly

Declaring a variable implicitly means that you don't tell VBA about the variable until you use it. When you declare the variable, you assign a value to it. You don't need to use any of the keywords, and you don't usually specify the data type—you let VBA figure the type out for itself.

Try this quick example of declaring a variable implicitly:

1. At the top of the Code window, comment out the Option Explicit statement by typing an apostrophe before it. You need to do this because this statement prevents you from using implicit declarations.

   ```
   'Option Explicit
   ```

2. In your WMME_Variables_1 macro, comment out the Dim line:

   ```
   'Dim strText As String
   ```

3. Click in the macro, and then press F5 to run it.

Again, you'll see the message box. But this time, the strText = line has declared the variable implicitly, because there's no explicit declaration.

Now try uncommenting the Option Explicit statement and see what happens:

1. Delete the apostrophe you typed before Option Explicit at the top of the Code window.

2. Click in the macro and press F5 to run it. You'll see the "Variable not defined" message shown here. This means that VBA is set to require variable declarations, but you've missed a declaration.

> **Microsoft Visual Basic**
>
> ⚠ Compile error:
>
> Variable not defined
>
> OK   Help

3. Click OK to dismiss the Compile Error message box. VBA selects the offending variable so that you can fix the problem.

4. Uncomment the Dim statement by deleting the apostrophe before it, and then run the macro. This time, it will run correctly.

WHY YOU SHOULD DECLARE VARIABLES EXPLICITLY

Earlier in this book, I recommended that you switch on the Require Variable Declaration check box on the Editor tab of the Visual Basic Editor's Options dialog box (choose Tools | Options). This setting forces you to declare all the variables you use explicitly and usually is a great help in keeping your code shipshape.

When you declare each variable explicitly, VBA knows about all the variables you're using and (usually) what type of data each is supposed to contain. This helps you in four ways:

■ When you type the name of a variable you've declared, VBA's automatic-completion features can help you to complete it.

■ It's easier to identify all the variables you've created (especially if you put the declarations at the beginning of the macro).

■ If you try to declare a new variable that has the same name as an existing variable, VBA warns you. With implicit declarations, VBA simply assigns the new value you give to the variable, overwriting its previous contents.

■ If you try to put the wrong type of data in a variable, VBA can often warn you.

There's no downside to declaring variables explicitly apart from having to be a tad more organized.

The Dim keyword is short for "dimension," in the sense of "reserve space for": "dimension such-and-such variable as an Integer" and so on.

Set the Variable's Scope and Lifetime

After the variable's name, the second thing you need to choose is the scope of the variable. *Scope* means the area of VBA in which you can use the variable.

You can use three different scopes: procedure scope, private scope, and public scope.

Declare a Variable with Procedure Scope

Procedure scope is the default scope. It means you can use the variable only within the macro (the VBA procedure) that declares it. This is the scope you'll normally want to use unless you need to use data from one macro in another.

To declare a variable with procedure scope, use the Dim keyword within a macro, just as you did earlier in this chapter—for example:

```
Dim strText As String
```

The variable retains its data only while the macro is running. As soon as the macro ends, VBA empties the memory that contained the variable.

Declare a Variable with Private Scope

Private scope is the next-wider scope. It creates a variable you can use in all the macros within the same module. A variable with private scope keeps its value as long as the VBA project (the Word template or document) that declares it is open.

To declare a private variable, you use the Private keyword and put the variable declaration in the declarations area at the top of the code module, after the Option Explicit statement and before any macro. Figure 7-1 shows an example.

You can also create a variable with private scope by using the Dim keyword at the beginning of the module rather than within a procedure. Don't do this, though—use the Private keyword instead, because it makes your code much clearer.

```
Normal - WMME_Chapter_7 (Code)
(General)                    ▼   WMME_
      Option Explicit

      Private strTown As String

      Sub WMME_Variables_2()
```

Figure 7-1 Place your private variables in the declarations area at the beginning of the code module.

Try this example of creating a private variable:

1. Click below the Option Explicit declaration at the beginning of the WMME_Chapter_7 module and declare a private variable named strTown of the String data type like this:

```
Private strTown As String
```

2. On the following line, type this macro, which assigns the text "Oakland" to the strTown variable:

```
Sub WMME_Variables_2()
    strTown = "Oakland"
End Sub
```

3. Click below that macro and type this macro, which displays a message box containing the contents of the strTown variable:

```
Sub WMME_Variables()
    MsgBox strTown
End Sub
```

4. Click in the WMME_Variables_2 macro and press F5 to run it. Nothing appears to happen, but VBA assigns the text to the variable.

5. Click in the WMME_Variables macro and press F5 to run it. VBA displays the message box with "Oakland" in it.

6. Click the OK button to dismiss the message box.

As you can see from this simple example, the private variable keeps its data and is available to all the macros in a module.

Declare a Variable with Public Scope

Public scope is the widest scope and makes the variable available to all the macros in all the modules in the project. Like a private variable, a variable with public scope keeps its value as long as the VBA project (the Word template or document) that declares it is open.

MEMO

When you edit a macro, VBA has to compile the code again before it can run. When VBA recompiles the code, it clears the values of all private and public variables. So if you find that your private variables have suddenly forgotten their values, it's usually because you have edited a macro.

Public variables are useful for sharing data between different modules.

You declare a public variable in much the same way as a private variable, except that you use the Public keyword instead of the Private keyword. You put the declaration in the declarations area at the top of any code module in the project.

Try this example of creating a public variable:

1. Click below the Option Explicit declaration and the Private strTown declaration at the beginning of the WMME_Chapter_7 module and declare a public variable named strProjectCode of the String data type:

    ```
    Public strProjectCode As String
    ```

2. On the following line, type this macro, which displays an input box prompting the user to type the project code and stores the user's answer in the strProjectCode variable:

    ```
    Sub WMME_Variables_3()
        strProjectCode = InputBox("Enter the project code:")
    End Sub
    ```

3. Don't run this macro just yet, because you need to create another macro that will test its output. Double-click the WMME_Chapter_7_2 module to open its code sheet, and then create this macro in it:

    ```
    Sub WMME_Variables_4()
        MsgBox strProjectCode
    End Sub
    ```

4. Now you're all set. Arrange the Code windows so that you can see both those modules. For example, choose Window | Tile Vertically or Window | Tile Horizontally.

5. Click in the WMME_Chapter_7 module, click in the WMME_Variables_3 macro, and then press F5 to run it. VBA displays the input box.

6. Type some text for the project code, and then press ENTER or click OK. VBA stores the string you typed in the strProjectCode variable.

MEMO

Use static variables to keep data that you'll need to use within the same macro but not in other macros. For example, the first time the user runs a macro in a Word session, you may need to gather relevant information from them. By storing this information in static variables, you can either avoid asking for it again in the same Word session or automatically insert the information in the fields of a userform so that the user can check it and approve it without needing to enter it again.

7. Click in the WMME_Chapter_7_2 module, click in the WMME_Variables_4 macro, and then press F5 to run it. VBA displays the message box with the text you typed.

As this example shows, the public variable keeps the data you assigned to it and is available to all the macros in a project.

Create Static Variables

The last type of variable is the *static* variable, which keeps its value between calls to the macro that declares it. Like a public variable, a static variable keeps its value as long as the project (the document or template) is open; but like a procedure-scope variable, a static variable is available only to the macro that declared it.

To declare a static variable, use the Static keyword just as you would use the Dim keyword. For example, the following statement declares a static variable named intPayments of the Integer data type:

```
Static intPayments As Integer
```

107

DEALING WITH "AMBIGUOUS NAME" ERRORS

As you learned earlier in this chapter, each variable's name must be unique within its scope, so that VBA knows which variable you're referring to. This is seldom a problem with procedure-scope variables, especially if you declare all your variables at the beginning of a macro, because you'll be able to see which variables you've created and avoid reusing any of the names.

But when you create public and private variables, it's much easier to reuse a variable name unintentionally. When you do this, VBA displays the Compile Error: Ambiguous Name Detected dialog box shown here, giving you the name of the offending macro.

Microsoft Visual Basic

Compile error:

Ambiguous name detected: WMME_Variables_3

OK   Help

Click the OK button, go to the macro, and change the variable name.

THE EASY WAY

Which types of variables you need depends on what you're doing in your macros. If you mostly create individual macros to sort out problems in Word, you may need to use only procedure-scope variables. Don't feel you need to create private, public, or static variables unless your macros actually need them.

MEMO

The most useful data types for writing macros in Word tend to be the String, Object, Integer, Boolean, and Date data types—but it depends very much on what your macros are doing.

Set the Variable's Data Type

The last decision you need to make when declaring a variable is its data type. You've been easing informally into using data types so far in this chapter, declaring String variables and Integer variables. Now it's time to lay out exactly what these terms mean.

The *data type* controls the type of data that the variable can hold. For example, if you've declared a variable as being of the Integer data type, it can hold only integers (whole numbers). If you try to store a string of text in the variable, you get an error, because it's not an integer.

Table 7-1 explains the data types you can use in VBA.

Decide Whether to Declare the Variable Type

Even if you set VBA to force you to declare each variable explicitly, you don't need to declare the variable's type. For example, instead of using the As keyword to declare the intCounter variable as being of the Integer data type, like this,

```
Dim intCounter As Integer
```

you can simply declare the variable explicitly without stating the data type, like this:

```
Dim intCounter
```

When you do this, VBA creates a variable of the Variant data type and gives it the Empty subtype (Variant/Empty). As soon as you assign data to the variable, VBA gives the variable the data subtype that best matches the data. For example, if you assign an integer value, VBA gives the variable the Variant/Integer subtype. And if you then assign a string of text, VBA gives the variable the Variant/String subtype.

This is flexible, but it takes more memory (which isn't usually a problem; see the upcoming sidebar "Why You Shouldn't Worry About Memory") and it enables you to assign the "wrong" type of data to a variable. In the previous example, the variable changes from a Variant/Integer to a Variant/String.

Data Type	A Variable That Can Contain	Suggested Abbreviation	Example
Boolean	Only True or False.	bln	True
Byte	An integer from 0 to 255 (inclusive).	byt	128
Currency	A positive or negative number that can have up to 15 digits before the decimal point and 4 digits after it.	cur	83929.2987
Date	A floating-point number that has the date before the decimal point and the time after it.	dte	34567.25
Decimal	An unsigned integer (not plus or minus) scaled by a power of 10. This data type is only available as a subtype of the Variant data type, not as a data type on its own.	N/A	4.825^{12}
Double	A floating-point number in either the range -1.79769313486232^{308} to -4.94065645841247^{-324} or the range 1.79769313486232^{208} to 4.94065645841247^{-324}.	dbl	2.8^{28}
Integer	A whole number from −32,768 to 32,767.	int	4096
Long	A whole number from −2,147,483,648 to 2,147,483,647.	lng	152,163
Object	A reference to a VBA object.	obj	(A document or paragraph)
Single	A floating-point number in either the range -3.40282^{-338} to -1.401298^{-45} or the range 1.401298^{-45} to 3.402823^{38}.	sng	1.4882^{25}
String	A string of text, either variable length or fixed length.	str	"Industry"
Variant	Any type of data except for a fixed-length string.	var	(See later in this chapter)

Table 7-1   VBA's Data Types for Variables

MEMO

Single means a single-precision floating-point number; *Double* means a double-precision floating-point number. These terms have to do with the way that computers handle the number. If you use these data types, you just need to make sure the values you're using are in the correct ranges.

If you try to perform math operations with the string, you'll get an error that you could have avoided by specifying the data type in the first place (which would have prevented the change of subtype).

Really the only reason to avoid declaring the data type is that you don't know what data type to use. But you can find it out quickly, as discussed next.

Find Out What Data Type Your Data Is

If some of the descriptions in Table 7-1 seem confusing, try using this easy way to find out what data type a particular piece of data is:

1. Create a macro to use:

    ```
    Sub WMME_Finding_Data_Type()

    End Sub
    ```

2. Declare the variable as a Variant. For example, declare a variable named myVariable:

    ```
    Dim myVariable As Variant
    ```

3. Assign to myVariable the data you want to check:

    ```
    myVariable = 44887289291.89129
    ```

4. Choose View | Locals Window to display the Locals window (shown in action in Figure 7-2). This window shows you the contents of variables and expressions you're using.

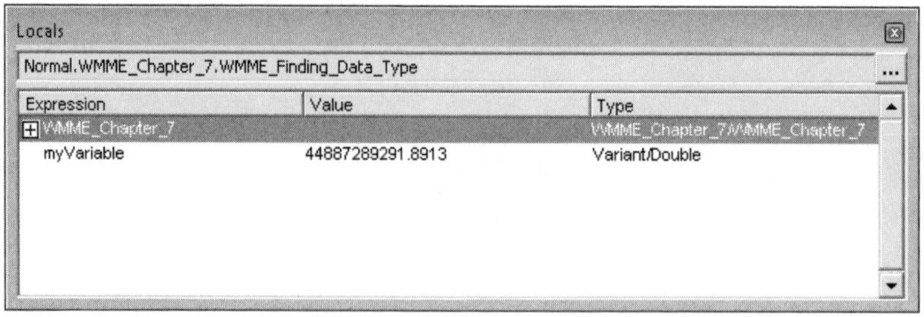

Figure 7-2 The Locals window shows you the contents and data type of variables your macros are using.

WHY YOU SHOULDN'T WORRY ABOUT MEMORY

Different variables take up different amounts of memory. For example, a Byte variable takes up 1 byte, a Boolean variable takes up 2 bytes, an Object variable takes up 4 bytes, and a Decimal integer takes up 12 bytes.

Professional programmers need to worry about the amount of memory their code uses, though not as much as they used to have to worry in the early days of computing, when memory was in short supply and every byte was precious. These days, any PC that can run Office 2007 at an acceptable speed should be able to handle all the variables you throw at it.

If you're only doing a small amount of programming in VBA, you shouldn't need to worry about the amount of memory variables take. The only exception is if you create many String variables or Variant variables and assign large amounts of text to them. In this case, the variables occupy a bit more memory than the text, which can add up to a significant amount if you create very many variables. But in all likelihood, you won't need to do this.

MEMO

There's one exception: If the data type is Decimal, you can't create a separate variable. Instead, leave the variable as a Variant and let VBA use the Variant/Decimal subtype for you.

5. Click in the macro and press F8 twice to execute the two statements.

6. Look at the myVariable line in the Locals window. The Type column shows the data subtype VBA is using within the Variant variable. You can use the corresponding data type for the variable. In the example, the variable is a Variant/Double, so you can declare the variable as a Double:

```
Dim dblMyLargeNumber As Double
```

7. Press F8 again to finish executing the macro.

Create Constants

A *constant* is a set value that you can use easily throughout your macros. You've already seen some of the constants that VBA itself uses, such as the vbYesNo constant you use for displaying Yes/No message boxes, but you may also need to create your own constants.

Like variables, constants can have procedure scope, private scope, or public scope:

- **Procedure scope**   Lets you use the constant only in the macro that declares it

- **Private scope**   Lets you use the constant anywhere in the module that declares it

- **Public scope**   Lets you use the constant anywhere in the project that declares it

To declare a constant, you use the Const statement like this:

```
[Public/Private] Const constantname [As type] = expression
```

Here's what that means:

- **[Public/Private]**   These are optional keywords that let you make the constant public or private. As with variables, you put public and private constant declarations in the declarations area at the top of the code sheet (before the first macro).

- **Const *constantname***   The Const keyword creates the constant with the name given by *constantname*. The naming rules are the same as for variables (see the sidebar "Learn the Rules for Naming Your Variables," earlier in this chapter).

- **[As *type*]**   The As keyword makes the constant the data type you give. Declaring the data type is optional, but it's always a good idea. You can use the same data types as for variables.

- **= *expression***   You assign the value to the constant by typing an equal sign followed by the value.

Try this quick example of creating a constant and using it immediately:

1. Create a macro to use:

   ```
   Sub WMME_Constants()

   End Sub
   ```

2. Type the following statement to declare a procedure-scope constant named conExchangeRate of the Currency data type and assign a value to it:

   ```
   Const conExchangeRate As Currency = 1.7734
   ```

3. Add a message box to display the result of the constant multiplied by 50:

   ```
   MsgBox conExchangeRate * 50
   ```

4. Click in the macro and press F5 to run it. You'll see the message box giving the result of the calculation.

Find the VBA Objects You Need

To take actions in your macros, you must identify the VBA objects that you need to manipulate. For example, when you need to create a new document, you need to work with the Documents collection; and when you work with a paragraph of text, you need to use the appropriate Paragraph object. This chapter shows you how to find the objects you need, using the fastest and easiest ways that VBA offers.

Get an Overview of the Tools You Can Use

VBA provides four main tools that you can use to find objects:

- **Help files** VBA comes with comprehensive Help files that you can search to find the objects, properties, and methods you need. Among the most useful parts of the Help files are the diagrams of the Word object model, which shows the various objects and the hierarchy in which they all fit together.

- **Macro Recorder**   As you've seen earlier in this book, you can record a macro by turning on the Macro Recorder and performing the actions you want to record. You can then examine the macro's code and see which VBA objects are involved. This is quick, easy, and often very effective. Many people view the Macro Recorder as strictly an entry-level tool, but that's their loss.

- **Object Browser**   The Object Browser is a tool for searching through objects in VBA and finding the ones you need. It's a bit forbidding at first, but it's a highly useful tool.

- **List Properties/Methods feature**   This feature, which you've met earlier in this book, lets you see the objects contained in an object whose name you've typed in code.

Understand What the Word Object Model Is

The Word object model is the logical arrangement in which Word's various objects fit together. By looking at the Help files' diagrams of the various parts of the object model, you can get an idea of which VBA objects there are and how to reach the ones you need to manipulate.

The easiest way to get an overview of the Word object model is to open the Word Object Model Maps in VBA Help. Follow these steps:

1. In the Visual Basic Editor, choose Help | Microsoft Visual Basic Help to open the Word Help window at the Word Developer topic.

2. In the Browse Word Developer Help list, click the Word Object Model Reference link to reach the Word Object Model Reference page.

3. Click the Word Object Model Maps link to display the Word Object Model Maps screen.

4. Click the Word Application Object Model Map to display the Word Application Object Model Map. Figure 8-1 shows the top part of this map.

5. Click an object to see its details.

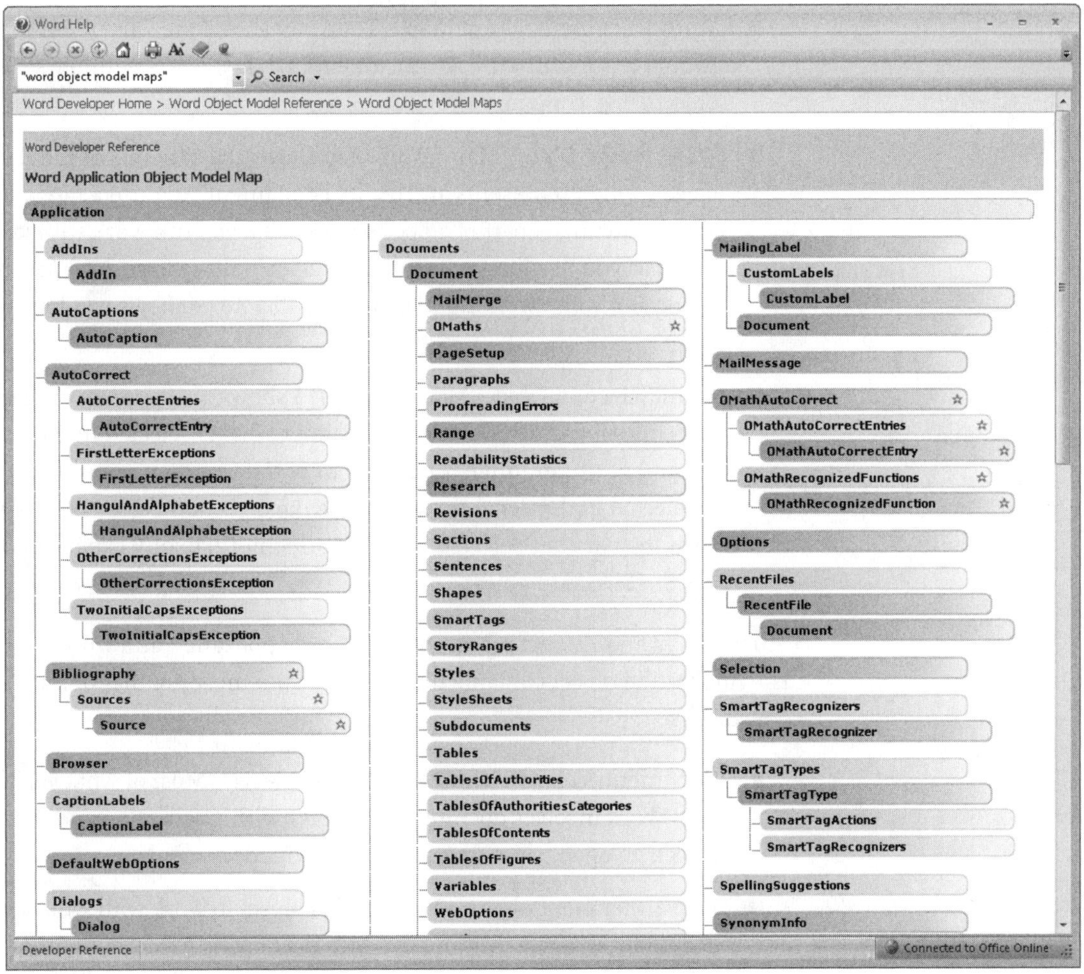

Figure 8-1   The Word Application Object Model Map shows you how the many objects are arranged in the Word application. You can click a box to jump to that object.

From the Word Object Model Maps screen, you can access four maps:

- **Word Application Object Model Map**   This map gives you an overview of the whole of the Word application.

- **Word Document Object Map**   This map shows the Document object (which represents an open document), all the objects within it, and the objects they contain.

- **Word Range Object Map**   This map shows the contents of the Range object, which represents an area in a document. You use a range in VBA to identify a part of a document so that you can work with it, much as you use the keyboard and mouse pointer to select a part of a document when working interactively. Chapter 9 shows you how to use ranges.

- **Word Selection Object Map**   This map shows the contents of the Selection object, which represents either what is selected in the document (for example, a paragraph) or the insertion point (if nothing is selected in the document). You use the Selection object to work with what the user has selected in the document. Chapter 9 explains how to use the Selection object.

The Application object represents the Word application as a whole. The Application object contains many objects, but these are the four you'll probably use most:

- **Documents collection and Document objects**   Most of what you'll do with Word involves documents, so you use this collection and these objects to open, close, save, and work with documents.

- **ActiveDocument object**   You use this object to work with whichever document is active, without needing to know its name.

- **Selection object**   You use this object to work with whatever the user has selected in the active document.

- **Options object**   This object lets you set most of the options in Word, including those that appear in the Word Options dialog box.

As you'll see if you look at the Word Application Object Model Map, the object model is arranged as a sort of tree diagram with the Application object as the root. To reach an object contained in another object, you normally drill down through the containing object to reach the object inside it. For example, the Application object contains the Documents collection, so you can reach the Documents collection by going through the Application object like this:

```
Application.Documents(1).TrackRevisions = False
```

To avoid you having to go through the Application object every time you do something in Word with VBA, the object model exposes various *creatable objects* that you can access without specifying the Application object. The Documents collection is a creatable object, so you can access it directly like this:

```
Documents(1).TrackRevisions = False
```

You'll learn much more about Word's objects and how to manipulate them in the remaining chapters of this book.

This section has given you a sideways introduction to the first way of finding the objects you need in Word: the VBA Help files. The next section tells you more about them.

Find an Object Using the Help Files

VBA includes detailed Help files you can use to find the objects you need, either by using the maps of the Word object model explained in the previous section or by searching for them.

You can open Help in any of these ways:

- Choose Help | Microsoft Visual Basic Help in the Visual Basic Editor. This opens the Word Help window at the Word Developer topic. From there, you can either browse the topics or click in the Search box, type a term, and click the Search button.

- Place the insertion point in a term you've entered in the Code window and press F1. This lets you jump directly to the Help page for the term you clicked.

- Type a term in the Search box in the Visual Basic Editor and press ENTER. The Word Help window shows a list of results. Click the result you want.

The VBA Help files include a wide variety of information, including examples and links to related objects. One of the most useful items is the Object Members list that you'll find in the See Also box on many pages. This lets you view a full list of the properties and methods available for the object.

Find Objects Using the Macro Recorder

Often, the easiest way to find out which objects you need to work with is by using the Macro Recorder. You turn it on, take actions interactively in the Word user interface to perform the tasks you want to automate, and then turn it off. You open the macro's code for editing in the Visual Basic Editor and see which objects VBA has used.

There are a couple of drawbacks. You'll see one in a moment, and I'll mention the other later in this chapter.

Record a Macro with the Macro Recorder

Try this example of using the Macro Recorder to find out how to turn off the Replace Text As You Type feature in AutoCorrect. Follow these steps:

1. Switch to Word (or launch it if it's not already running).

2. Open the Record Macro dialog box in one of these ways:

   - Click the Record Macro button on the status bar:

- Click the Developer tab, go to the Code group, and click the Record Macro button.

3. In the Macro Name text box, type a name for the macro that will enable you to identify the macro for deleting when you no longer need it. (You can leave the default name—Macro 1, Macro 2, or whatever—if you prefer.)

4. Make sure the Store Macro In drop-down list is set to All Documents (Normal.dotm).

5. Leave the Description field blank if you're planning to delete the macro.

6. Click OK. Word closes the Record Macro dialog box and starts recording the macro.

7. Click the Office button, and then click Word Options to open the Word Options dialog box.

8. In the left panel, click the Proofing category to display the Proofing options.

9. In the AutoCorrect Options area, click the AutoCorrect Options button to open the AutoCorrect dialog box.

10. On the AutoCorrect tab, clear the Replace Text As You Type check box.

11. Click the OK button to close the AutoCorrect dialog box.

12. Click the OK button to close the Word Options dialog box.

13. Stop recording the macro in one of these ways:

    - Click the Stop Recording button on the status bar:

      | Page: 1 of 1 | Words: 0 | English (United States) | ■ |

      A macro is currently recording. Click to stop recording.

    - Click the Developer tab, go to the Code group, and click the Stop Recording button.

Open the Macro You Recorded

Now open the macro you recorded and view its contents:

1. Open the Macros dialog box in one of these ways:

   ■ Press ALT-F8.

   ■ Click the Developer tab, go to the Code group, and then click the Macros button.

2. In the Macro Name list box, click the macro's name, and then click the Edit button. Word launches or activates the Visual Basic Editor, which opens the NewMacros module, where you can find your macro.

When you open the macro for turning off the Replace Text As You Type feature, you'll see a huge slab of code that starts like this:

```
Sub Macro1()
'
' Macro1 Macro
'
'
    With Options
        .AutoFormatAsYouTypeApplyHeadings = False
        .AutoFormatAsYouTypeApplyBorders = True
        .AutoFormatAsYouTypeApplyBulletedLists = True
        .AutoFormatAsYouTypeApplyNumberedLists = True
        .AutoFormatAsYouTypeApplyTables = True
        .AutoFormatAsYouTypeReplaceQuotes = True
        .AutoFormatAsYouTypeReplaceSymbols = True
        .AutoFormatAsYouTypeReplaceOrdinals = True
        .AutoFormatAsYouTypeReplaceFractions = True
        .AutoFormatAsYouTypeReplacePlainTextEmphasis = False
        .AutoFormatAsYouTypeReplaceHyperlinks = True
        .AutoFormatAsYouTypeFormatListItemBeginning = True
        .AutoFormatAsYouTypeDefineStyles = False
        .TabIndentKey = True
    End With
    With AutoCorrect
```

```
With AutoCorrect
        .CorrectInitialCaps = True
        .CorrectSentenceCaps = True
        .CorrectDays = True
        .CorrectCapsLock = True
        .ReplaceText = False
        .ReplaceTextFromSpellingChecker = True
        .CorrectKeyboardSetting = False
        .DisplayAutoCorrectOptions = True
        .CorrectTableCells = True
End With
...
```

I've deleted the second half of the code, because it's neither pretty nor helpful.

This illustrates the main problem you'll find with using the Macro Recorder to find objects: When you use a dialog box, the Macro Recorder doesn't know exactly which setting you're interested in, so it records all of them. You then have to go through them and find the one you want.

Here, the object we want is the AutoCorrect object, and the setting is ReplaceText = False. Once we know this, we can simplify the macro to this:

```
Sub WMME_Turn_Off_AutoCorrect()
    AutoCorrect.ReplaceText = False
End Sub
```

When you've found the code you want, either copy it to a macro of your own or simply note down what you need to know. Then delete the recorded macro in one of these ways:

- **Code window**   Select the macro's code, and then press DELETE.

- **Visual Basic Editor**   Choose Tools | Macros, click the macro's name in the Macros dialog box, and then click the Delete button.

- **Word**   Press ALT-F8 to open the Macros dialog box, click the macro's name, and then click the Delete button.

WHY YOU MAY NEED TO CHANGE THE SELECTION OBJECT

When you record macros that involve you doing things in a document (as opposed to choosing settings, as in the previous example), you'll find that VBA often uses the Selection object.

The Selection object represents whatever the user has selected in Word—for example, a word, a sentence, or a paragraph. If nothing is actually selected as we humans understand it, VBA still identifies a Selection object. It represents the position of the insertion point and is called a "collapsed selection."

When you're recording macros that you'll play back, using the Selection object is fine, because the macros will usually run as needed. Sometimes a macro will fail if the user runs it on a different type of selection than for which it was recorded. For example, if you recorded the macro to manipulate the cells in a table, it won't work with a different object (such as a picture) that doesn't have cells.

But when you're using the Macro Recorder to find the objects you need for writing code, you'll often need to switch from the Selection object to another object. For example, if you use the Macro Recorder to discover the commands needed to format text using VBA, the recorded code will use the Selection object. But you'll often need to use another object instead, such as a Range object within a Paragraph object in a Document object. (You'll learn more about these objects later in this book.)

Find Objects Using the Object Browser

The Object Browser is a tool for searching through objects in VBA to find the ones you need. The Object Browser is powerful and takes some getting used to, but if you follow the example in this section, you'll get the hang of it in just a few minutes.

Open the Object Browser

You can open the Object Browser in any of these ways from the Visual Basic Editor:

■ Press F2.

■ Click the Object Browser button on the Standard toolbar:

■ Choose View | Object Browser.

Figure 8-2 shows the Object Browser open as a floating (undocked) window.

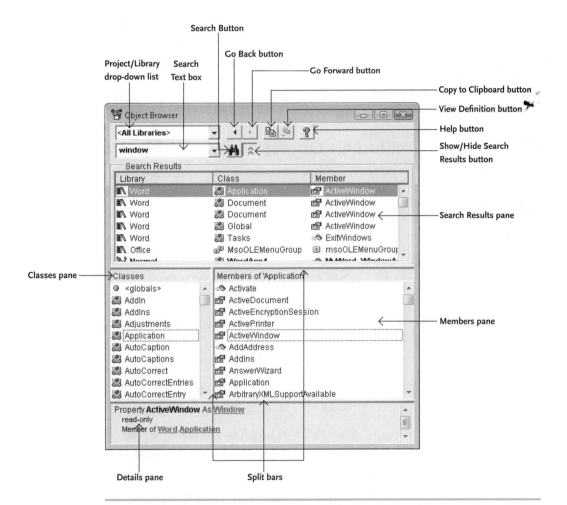

Figure 8-2   The Object Browser is a great tool for digging through the objects, properties, and methods that VBA provides.

MEMO

You can resize the Object Browser by dragging any of its corners or borders. You can also resize the Search Results pane, the Classes pane, the Members pane, and the Details pane by dragging the split bars between them. And if you want to hide the Search Results pane to give more space to the Classes pane and Members pane, click the Show/Hide Search Results button.

If the Object Browser opens as a window docked within the Visual Basic Editor window, taking up all of the space where the Code window normally appears, you can display it as a separate window by clicking the Restore Window button in the upper-right corner of the Visual Basic Editor window, as shown here. Double-click the Object Browser's title bar or click its Maximize button if you want to maximize it again.

The easiest way to see what the different components of the Object Browser do is by using it to find an object. You'll do that next.

Find an Object with the Object Browser

Despite the Object Browser's name, the quickest way to find the object you need is usually to search for it. Once you've found it, you can browse the surrounding objects.

In this example, you'll search the Object Browser to find the object you use for setting the margins in a document. Follow these steps:

1. Open the Object Browser as discussed in the previous section. For example, press F2.

2. In the Project/Library drop-down list, choose Word to display the contents of the Word library. Figure 8-3 shows the Object Browser with the Word library selected.

3. Click in the Search Text box and type the term you want to search for: **margins**.

4. Click the Search button. The Object Browser displays the list of matching results in the Search Results box (see Figure 8-4).

5. In the Search Results box, click the object whose contents you want to view. The Classes pane displays the classes in that object, and the Members pane displays the individual elements.

If you're not sure exactly what you're looking for, you can use the wildcards **?** (which represents any one character) and ***** (which represents any group of characters) in the Object Browser. If you want to restrict your searches to whole words rather than words that contain your search term, right-click the Search button and choose Find Whole Word Only from the context menu. The Visual Basic Editor puts a check mark next to this option, indicating it is switched on.

Figure 8-3   You'll recognize some of the objects in the Word library in the Object Browser.

If you go astray on your searches, click the Go Back button to retrace your steps. Once you've gone back, you can click the Go Forward button to go forward again if you need to.

6. Once you've found an item you're interested in, click it to display its details in the Details pane. You can also click one of the following to take other actions:

■ **Copy to Clipboard**   Click this button to copy the item you've selected to the Clipboard so that you can paste it into your code. Copying saves any amount of remembering and retyping.

■ **View Definition**   If you've selected an object containing VBA code, you can click this button to display a Code window containing the object's code. This capability lets you use the

127

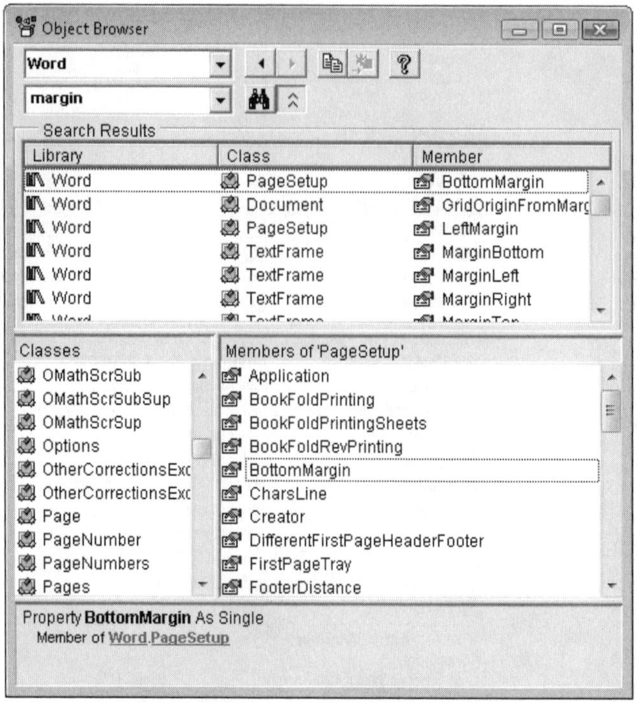

Figure 8-4   Look through the items in the Search Results box for an object that looks promising.

Object Browser to browse your own code. You'll need to select Normal in the Project/Library drop-down list to see the contents of the Normal template. Select Project in the Project/Library drop-down list to see the contents of other open projects.

■   **Links**   Click a link in the Details pane to display the linked term. You can then continue browsing from there.

Close the Object Browser

When you've finished using the Object Browser, click its close button (the ×button) to close it. Annoyingly, you can't close the Object Browser by pressing F2 again—that keyboard shortcut only displays the window.

Find an Object Using the List Properties/Methods Feature

As you've seen in the earlier chapters, the List Properties/Methods feature automatically displays a list of properties and methods for an object you've entered in code. For example, when you type **Document**. (including that period), the List Properties/Methods feature displays a list of the properties and methods for the Document object.

This makes the List Properties/Methods feature a useful tool for finding the objects you need—as long as they're contained within an object you already know. In other words, you need to know the starting point.

Try this example to find the object that lets you zoom the view on a window. Because VBA starts at the outside like a set of Russian nesting dolls, you start with the window. As you've seen earlier, VBA uses the Window object to represent a window and uses the ActiveWindow object to represent whichever window is currently active.

Follow these steps:

1. In the Visual Basic Editor, open the Immediate window in one of these ways:

   - Choose View | Immediate Window.

   - Press CTRL-G.

   - Click the Immediate Window button on the Debug toolbar:

2. Type **activewindow.** (including the period) to display the list of properties and methods.

MEMO

The Immediate window is a window you can use for testing one statement at a time.

3. Type **v** to jump to the first item beginning with *V* in the list (see Figure 8-5).

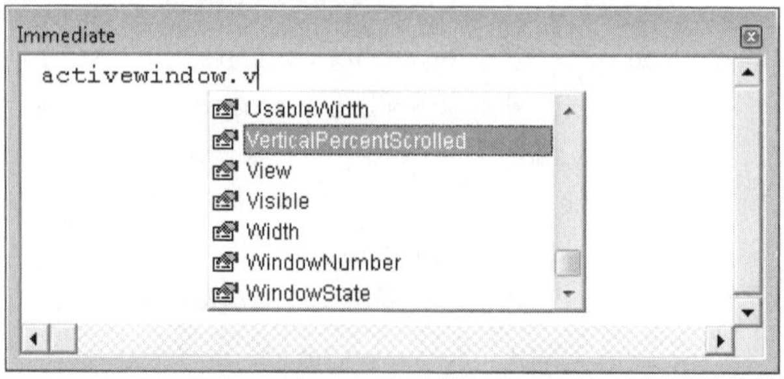

Figure 8-5   The Immediate window is a scratchpad for working with code.

4. Type **i** to select the View item in the list and press . (period) to enter it and display its list of properties and methods.

5. Type **z** to jump to the first item beginning with *Z* in the list—the Zoom item (see Figure 8-6).

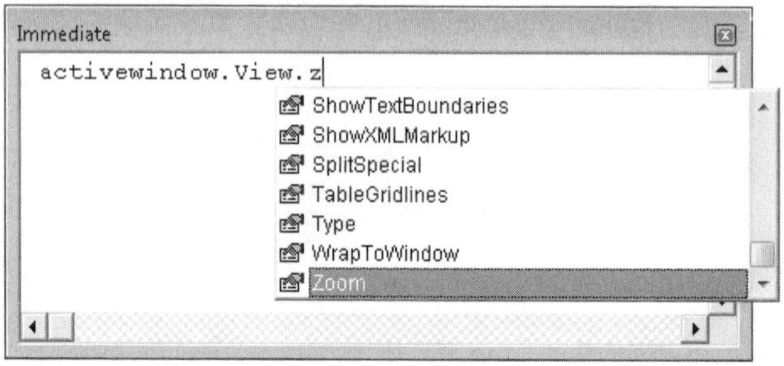

Figure 8-6   The List Properties/Methods feature lets you drill down through the objects to the one you want.

6. Type . (period) to enter the Zoom item and display its list of properties and methods (see Figure 8-7).

7. Select the item you want: PageFit.

8. Press = to enter PageFit and to display the list of constants you can use: wdPageFitBestFit, wdPageFitFullPage, wdPageFitNone, and wdPageFitTextFit.

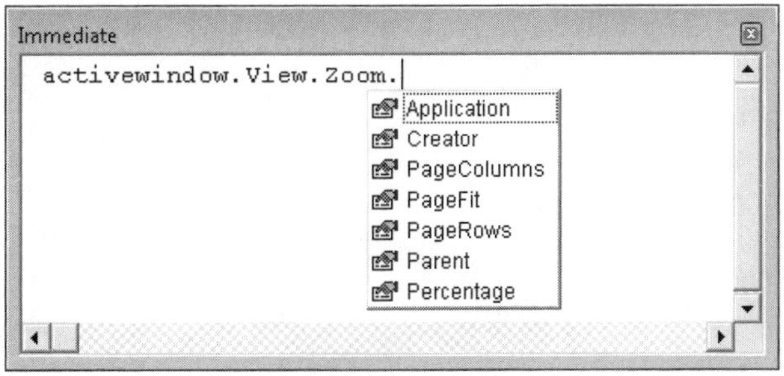

Figure 8-7 Finally you reach the properties and methods you need.

9. Select the wdPageFitFullPage item and press ENTER. The full statement appears in the Immediate window.

10. Press ENTER to execute the statement. Word zooms the active window so that the whole page is visible.

11. Click the Close button (the × button) to close the Immediate window.

Work with Text

If you're creating documents in Word, or even if you're just editing them, you'll probably spend a lot of time working with text. This chapter shows you how to do so quickly and effectively. You'll learn how to use the Selection object, which lets you work with the user's current selection in the document, and how to create and use ranges that allow you to manipulate any part of the document you choose. I'll also show you how to apply formatting via VBA and how to use Word's powerful Find and Replace features in your macros. First, though, a quick word on how VBA represents the text parts of a document.

Understand How VBA Represents Text

To VBA, a document is typically a sequence of Paragraph objects with other objects (such as Table objects) added to them. So when you're accessing the text in a document, you're usually working through a Paragraph object.

You access a Paragraph object through the Paragraphs collection. For example, to work with the first paragraph in the active document, you start a statement with ActiveDocument.Paragraphs(1).

VBA also lets you access a sentence by using the Sentences collection to identify the appropriate Sentence object. You can access a sentence

MEMO

Be careful with Sentence objects, because VBA's definition of a sentence isn't as clear as you might expect. For example, VBA treats a short paragraph that has no punctuation as a sentence, sending grammarians into apoplexy.

either directly through a Document object (for example, ActiveDocument. Sentences(1) gets you the first sentence in the active document) or through a paragraph (for example, Documents(1).Paragraphs(1).Range.Sentences(1) gets you the first sentence in the first paragraph in the first open document).

VBA represents each word as a Word object, which you access through the Words collection. You can access a word directly from a Document object or from another object that contains words, such as the Selection object or the Range object inside a Paragraph object.

Similarly, VBA represents each character as a Character object and gathers them in the Characters collection. You can access a single character either from a Document object or from another object that contains characters.

Going through the Document object is easy enough, but when you need to work with whatever the user has selected, you can use the Selection object instead. This is often very convenient, so we'll start there after getting you set up to work through this chapter.

Get Set Up to Work Through This Chapter

Follow these steps to open the Visual Basic Editor and create a new module in which you will work with text:

1. Open Microsoft Word if it's not already running. If it is running, close any open documents.

2. Press ALT-F11 to open the Visual Basic Editor.

3. If the Visual Basic Editor opens a Code window for a module you worked with recently, click the window's Close button (the × button) to close it.

4. Right-click the Normal template and then choose Insert | Module from the context menu to insert a new module in the Normal template.

5. Press F4 to put the focus in the Properties window.

6. Type **WMME_Chapter_9** as the new name for the module, replacing the default name (such as Module1), and then press ENTER to apply the change.

7. Press CTRL-G to open the Immediate window, which lets you execute single commands without having to put them in a macro.

8. If no document is open in Word, type **documents.add** and press ENTER to create a new document based on the Normal template. You'll use this text for some of the macros in this chapter. (If you opened Word in step 1, and Word created a blank document for you, use that document instead.)

Work with Text via the Selection Object

When you start working with VBA, you'll often find it convenient to use the Selection object, as you did in the macro you recorded and then edited at the beginning of this book. The Selection object represents the user's selection and is great for macros that the user runs to manipulate parts of documents. For example, if you create a macro that turns selected text into a pull quote, you'll typically need the user to pick the text and run the macro on it rather than picking the text programmatically.

MEMO

The Selection object is always in the active document. When you activate another document, the Selection object is then in that document. There's always a Selection object, even when nothing is selected and the insertion point appears between letters or on a blank paragraph.

Find the Details of the Current Selection

To find out the details of the current selection, you can use its Information property. This property gives you access to several dozen different pieces of information ranging from what type of Word item is selected to whether the selection is in a table. To find out about the Information property, you check the wdInformation constant for the appropriate piece of information. Table 9-1 tells you what you need to know.

wdInformation Constant	What It Tells You
General Information	
wdCapsLock	Whether Caps Lock is on (True).
wdNumLock	Whether Num Lock is on (True).
wdOverType	Whether Overtype mode is on (True).
wdRevisionMarking	Whether Track Changes (revision marking) is on (True).
wdSelectionMode	Whether the selection is normal (0), a selection in Extend mode (1), or a columnar selection (2).
wdZoomPercentage	The zoom percentage.
Information about the Selection and Insertion Point	
wdActiveEndAdjustedPageNumber	Which page the end of the selection is on. If you change the starting page number, this page number changes.
wdActiveEndPageNumber	Which page the end of the selection is on. This page number does not change if you change the starting page number.
wdActiveEndSectionNumber	Which section the end of the selection is in.
wdFirstCharacterColumnNumber	The character position of the selection's first character (the number of characters from the left margin). If the selection is collapsed, you get the number of the character to the right of the insertion point.
wdFirstCharacterLineNumber	The line number of the selection's first character in Print Layout view, Full Screen Reading view, and Print Preview. In Draft view, Outline view, or Web Layout view, returns −1.
wdFrameIsSelected	Whether the selection is a whole frame or text box (True).
wdHeaderFooterType	The type of header or footer the selection is in: not in a header or footer (−1); even-page header (0); odd-page header or the document's only header (1); even-page footer (2); odd-page footer or the document's only footer (3); first-page header (4); first-page footer (5).
wdHorizontalPosition-RelativeToPage	The number of twips (1/1440 inch) to the selection's left edge from the left edge of the page.
wdHorizontalPositionRelative-ToTextBoundary	The number of twips from the selection's left edge to the boundary of the text area.

Table 9-1   Information Available about the Selection Object

wdInformation Constant	What It Tells You
wdInCommentPane	Whether the selection is in a comment pane (True).
wdInEndnote	Whether the selection is in an endnote (True).
wdInFootnote	Whether the selection is in a footnote (True).
wdInFootnoteEndnotePane	Whether the selection is in a footnote or endnote (True).
wdInHeaderFooter	Whether the selection is in a header or footer (True).
wdInMasterDocument	Whether the selection is in a master document containing at least one subdocument (True).
wdInWordMail	Whether the selection is part of a WordMail send note (1), part of a WordMail read note (2), or not in WordMail (0).
wdNumberOfPagesInDocument	How many pages are in the document that contains the selection.
wdReferenceOfType	Whether the selection is before a footnote reference (1), an endnote reference (2), or a comment reference (3). Returns 0 if the selection isn't before a reference. Returns −1 if the selection includes a reference but also other items.
wdVerticalPositionRelativeToPage	The number of twips from the selection's top edge to the top of the page.
wdVerticalPositionRelative-ToTextBoundary	The number of twips from the selection's top to the boundary of the text area.
Information about Selections Inside Tables	
wdWithinTable	Whether the selection is in a table (True).
wdStartOfRangeColumnNumber	Which table column contains the selection's start.
wdEndOfRangeColumnNumber	Which table column contains the selection's end.
wdStartOfRangeRowNumber	Which table row contains the selection's start.
wdEndOfRangeRowNumber	Which table row contains the selection's end.
wdAtEndOfRowMarker	Whether the selection is at the end-of-row marker (True) or not (False). The end-of-row marker is the character that appears at the end of the row when you turn on the display of formatting marks.
wdMaximumNumberOfColumns	The maximum number of columns in any part of the selection.
wdMaximumNumberOfRows	The maximum number of rows in any part of the selection.

Table 9-1   Information Available about the Selection Object (*cont.*)

MEMO

Extend mode is an odd selection mode that you enter by pressing F8. Keep pressing F8 to select a word, sentence, paragraph, and so on, or press the character in text to which you want to extend the selection. (For example, press **w** to extend the selection to the next letter *w*.) A columnar selection is what you get if you ALT-drag down and across lines of text to select a block of characters.

Use the Information Property to Check Word Settings

To try using the Information property of the Selection object, click in the Code window for your WMME_Chapter_9 module and create the WMME_Selection_Information macro shown here:

```
Sub WMME_Selection_Information()
    If Selection.Information(wdRevisionMarking) = True Then
        ActiveDocument.TrackRevisions = False
    End If
    If Selection.Information(wdSelectionMode) = 1 Then
        Selection.ExtendMode = False
    End If
    If Selection.Information(wdOverType) = True Then
        Options.Overtype = False
    End If
End Sub
```

The WMME_Selection_Information macro uses the Information property of the Selection object to check three settings and turn them off if they're on:

■ First, it checks whether revision marking (Track Changes) is on.

■ Second, it checks whether Extend mode is on.

■ Third, it checks whether Overtype mode is on. (In Overtype mode, each character you type replaces the character to its right rather than pushing that character further along the document.)

Click in the macro and press F8 to step through it. Watch what happens. Then try turning on the settings the macro checks, and then test the macro again:

■ **Track Changes**   Press CTRL-SHIFT-E in Word.

■ **Extend mode**   Press F8 in Word.

■ **Overtype mode**   Choose Tools | Word Options, and then click the Advanced category. In the Editing Options list, select the Use Overtype Mode check box, and then click the OK button.

Use the Information Property to Check the Selection's Location

Next, try this example, which checks that the selection is not in a header, footer, footnote, endnote, or comment. If the selection is guilty of any of these offenses, the macro adds the relevant words to the message string (strMsg) and sets the Boolean variable blnProblem to True. If blnProblem is True at the end of the macro, VBA displays the message box announcing the problem.

```
Sub WMME_Selection_Information_2()

    Dim strMsg As String
    Dim blnProblem As Boolean

    strMsg = "Please run this macro in the main part " & _
             "of the document, not in "

    If Selection.Information(wdInHeaderFooter) = True Then
        strMsg = strMsg & "a header or footer."
        blnProblem = True
    End If

    If Selection.Information(wdInCommentPane) = True Then
        strMsg = strMsg & "a comment."
        blnProblem = True
    End If

    If Selection.Information(wdInEndnote) = True Then
        strMsg = strMsg & "an endnote."
        blnProblem = True
    End If

    If Selection.Information(wdInFootnote) = True Then
        strMsg = strMsg & "a footnote."
        blnProblem = True
    End If
```

```
        If blnProblem = True Then
            MsgBox strMsg, vbOKOnly + vbExclamation, _
                "Text Formatter Macro"
        End If

End Sub
```

With the insertion point in the main part of your Word document, click in this macro and press F8 to step through it. VBA evaluates all the conditions, finds them unmet, and displays no message box.

Next, position the insertion point in the header area of the document and try the macro again. This time, you'll get the message box, with the "not in a header or footer" message. Create a footnote, endnote, or comment; position the insertion point in that item's area (for example, the endnote area); and then run the macro again.

Insert and Delete Text in Documents

When you've determined that the macro is working with the type of selection it's designed to use, you'll often need to insert or delete text.

Insert Text at the Current Selection

The easiest way to insert text is by using the TypeText method of the Selection object. For example:

```
Selection.TypeText "Here is the report you were looking for."
```

Try opening the Immediate window (press CTRL-G), typing this statement, and then pressing ENTER. VBA types the text at the position of the insertion point in the document.

Insert Text Before or After the Current Selection

To insert text before a selection, you use the InsertBefore method. To insert text after a selection or range, you use the InsertAfter method. In the Immediate window, try this example, which inserts text before the current selection:

```
Selection.InsertBefore "Report prepared by Chris Jones"
```

MEMO

To insert a tab in a document, use the vbTab constant. For example, Selection .TypeText vbTab "types" a tab in the document. Similarly, you can "type" a carriage-return character by using the vbCr constant—but the TypeParagraph method is often easier.

When you press ENTER, you'll see this text appear in the Word document before the point where the insertion point was. You'll notice that Word extends the selection so that it includes the text you just inserted.

Insert a Paragraph

VBA gives you four methods for inserting a paragraph in a document:

- **TypeParagraph**   Types a paragraph at the selection

- **InsertParagraph**   Inserts the paragraph at the position of the selection and extends the selection to include the new paragraph

- **InsertParagraphAfter**   Inserts the paragraph after the selection and extends the selection to include the new paragraph

- **InsertParagraphBefore**   Inserts the paragraph before the selection and extends the selection to include the new paragraph

Format the Selection

What you'll often need to do with the selection is format it. We'll look at how to format text later in this chapter.

Delete the Selection

To delete the selection, simply use the Delete method. For example:

```
Selection.Delete
```

MEMO

If the selection has no contents, using the Delete method deletes the character to the right of the insertion point, as if you'd pressed DELETE when working interactively.

Deselect the Selection

After checking what the selection contains, you may need to deselect whatever it is. The easiest way to do this is to collapse the selection to either its starting point (using wdCollapseStart) or its ending point (using wdCollapseEnd). For example, this statement collapses the selection to its start, much as if you'd pressed LEFT ARROW in Word:

```
Selection.Collapse Direction:=wdCollapseStart
```

141

Another method is to set the start of the selection to the same place as the end of the selection (as in the next statement) or vice versa:

```
Selection.Start = Selection.End
```

Work with Text Through a Document Object

Working with the Selection object is handy when you want the macro's user to pick the text or other object to affect. In other macros, you can go through the ActiveDocument object or another Document object to tell VBA which part of the document you want to affect.

Using a Document object lets you work with a document that isn't the active document. For example, you can manipulate a document in the background, keeping the changes hidden from the user. You can also work with two or more different documents at the same time.

To access a document, you use the Documents collection and specify the document either by name or by its index number within the collection. For example, the following statement selects the first paragraph in the first document in the Documents collection:

```
Documents(1).Paragraphs(1).Range.Select
```

Usually when you're working with VBA, it's hard to know which document is Documents(1), so using the document's name is easier. For example, the following statement applies Heading 1 style to the first paragraph in the open document named Sales Figures.docx:

```
Documents("Sales Figures.docx").Paragraphs(1).Style = "Heading 1"
```

Work with Ranges

When you need to work with a particular part of a document, you can create a range that refers to it.

MEMO

If you need to perform several operations with the same part of a document, define a range for it, as discussed in the this section.

142

A *range* is simply an area of a document. When you create the range, you specify which part of the document it refers to. You can then use the range name to refer to that part of the document more easily. For example, you can create a range that refers to the first paragraph of a document, or the first five words in a particular paragraph in the document.

To create a range, you first declare an Object variable of the Range type. You then use the Range method of a Document object or the Range property of another object to assign the range to the Object variable.

That sounds complicated, but it's easy enough when you try it. Follow these steps:

1. In Word, open your Report Summary.docx document from your WMME folder.

2. In the Visual Basic Editor, click in the Code window for the WMME_Chapter_9 module, and create the stub for a macro by typing **Sub WMME_Ranges_1** and then pressing ENTER:

```
Sub WMME_Ranges_1()

End Sub
```

3. Inside the stub, start by declaring two Object variables of the Range type, one named rngTitle and the other named rngIntro:

```
Dim rngTitle As Range
Dim rngIntro As Range
```

4. Below those declarations, start a With statement that works with the Report Summary.docx document:

```
With Documents("Report Summary.docx")

End With
```

5. Inside the With statement, use a Set statement and the Range method of the Document object to assign to rngTitle a range that starts at

the beginning of the first paragraph and ends at the end of the first paragraph:

```
Set rngTitle = _
    .Range(Start:=.Paragraphs(1).Range.Start, _
    End:=.Paragraphs(1).Range.End)
```

6. After that (and still within the With statement), use another Set statement to assign to rngIntro the Range property of the second paragraph:

```
Set rngIntro = .Paragraphs(2).Range
```

7. On a line after the End With statement, add a MsgBox statement that will display the Text property of rngTitle and rngIntro, together with explanatory text:

```
MsgBox "Title: " & rngTitle.Text & vbCr & _
    "Intro: " & rngIntro.Text
```

Here's the full code of the macro for reference:

```
Sub WMME_Ranges_1()

    Dim rngTitle As Range
    Dim rngIntro As Range

    With Documents("Report Summary.docx")
        Set rngTitle = .Range(Start:=.Paragraphs(1).Range.Start, _
            End:=.Paragraphs(1).Range.End)
        Set rngIntro = .Paragraphs(2).Range
    End With

    MsgBox "Title: " & rngTitle.Text & vbCr & _
        "Intro: " & rngIntro.Text

End Sub
```

Step through the code by pressing F8. After you execute the first Set statement, move the mouse pointer over the rngTitle variable to display a ScreenTip showing the variable's contents; this gives you a quick confirmation that the code is working. When you execute the MsgBox statement, VBA displays a message box that shows you the text in both of the variables.

Apply Formatting and Styles

Once you've identified the part of the document you want to work with, you can format it via VBA with the same amount of control as you would have if you were working in the Word user interface. This section briefly shows you how to apply styles, paragraph formatting, and font formatting.

Apply Styles

As you'll know from working interactively with Word, using styles is the fastest and most efficient way of formatting your documents. By using styles rather than direct formatting, you can ensure consistency across your documents—and if you need to change the formatting of a style, the change carries through immediately to all the paragraphs to which you've applied the style.

To apply a paragraph style with VBA, set the Style property of the Paragraph object, Range object, or Selection object. For example, the following statement applies the Heading 1 style to the first paragraph in the Report Summary.docx document:

```
Documents("Report Summary.docx").Paragraphs(1).Style = "Heading 1"
```

To apply a character style, set the Style property of the appropriate object—for example, a word or a character. For example, the following statement applies the Subtle Emphasis style to the first word in the second paragraph of the active document:

```
ActiveDocument.Paragraphs(2).Range.Words(1).Style = _
    "Subtle Emphasis"
```

Apply Paragraph Formatting

Even if you apply a style to every paragraph, you will sometimes need to apply direct formatting for special effects. To apply paragraph formatting, you use the ParagraphFormat object for the appropriate Selection or Range object. The ParagraphFormat object has properties and methods that you'll recognize from working in the Paragraph dialog box in Word.

Try creating the following macro and running it with the Latest Report .docx document open:

```
Sub WMME_Paragraph_Formatting()
    With ActiveDocument.Paragraphs(3).Range.ParagraphFormat
        .Alignment = wdAlignParagraphCenter
        .KeepTogether = True
        .LineSpacingRule = wdLineSpaceAtLeast
        .LineSpacing = 18
    End With
End Sub
```

Here's what this macro does:

- The With statement makes the statements within it work with the ParagraphFormat object in the Range object in the third Paragraph object. In other words, it changes the formatting of the third paragraph.

- The .Alignment statement applies center alignment to the paragraph.

- The .KeepTogether statement sets Word to keep the lines of the paragraph together rather than letting them break from one page to another.

- The .LineSpacingRule statement sets the line spacing type to "at least" (wdLineSpaceAtLeast).

- The .LineSpacing statement then sets the number of points to use: 18.

Apply Font Formatting

If you need to apply font formatting directly to characters or words in a document, use the Font property of the object you want to format—for example, the Selection object or a Range object. This returns the Font object, which lets you access formatting options that will be familiar from Word's Font dialog box.

Try creating the following macro, selecting one or more words in your document, and then running the macro:

```
Sub WMME_Font_Formatting()
    With Selection.Font
        .Bold = True
        .Italic = False
        .Color = wdColorDarkBlue
        .Name = "Arial"
        .Size = "20"
        .SmallCaps = True
    End With
End Sub
```

Work with Find and Replace

Word's Find and Replace features are great for processing documents. You can control these features just as closely via VBA as you can when working interactively, searching for not only text or other content but also formatting and attributes.

Meet the Find Object

To work with Find via VBA, you use the Find object. Find has a wide variety of properties, of which Table 9-2 shows the most useful.

Meet the Replacement Object

To use Word's Replace feature in your macros, you work with the Replacement object. This object has five of the same properties as the Find

147

Find Property	Explanation
Font	The font formatting you're searching for.
Forward	The search direction: forward (True) or backward (False).
Found	Whether the search has found a match (True) or not (False).
Highlight	Whether the replacement text includes highlighting (True) or not (False).
MatchAllWordForms	Whether Word is searching for all word forms (True) or not (False).
MatchCase	Whether the search is case specific (True) or not (False).
MatchSoundsLike	Whether the search includes words that Word thinks sound like it (True) or not (False).
MatchWholeWord	Whether the search is for whole words only (True) or includes the search term within other words (False).
MatchWildcards	Whether the search uses wildcards (True) or not (False).
ParagraphFormat	The paragraph formatting you're searching for.
Replacement	Returns the Replacement object, which you use to specify the replacement text and formatting.
Style	A name or constant specifying the style you're searching for.
Text	The text you're searching for (or an empty string—""—if you're searching for formatting).
Wrap	Whether to continue ("wrap") a search if it starts anywhere other than the beginning of the document (for a forward search) or the end of the document (for a backward search). Use wdFindContinue to continue searching, wdFindStop to stop searching, and wdFindAsk to prompt the user whether to continue or stop.

Table 9-2   The Most Useful Properties of the Find Object

object (see Table 9-2): Font, Highlight, ParagraphFormat, Style, and Text. These properties work in the same way as described in Table 9-2 but affect the Replacement object rather than the Find object.

An Example of Finding Text

Click after the last macro in your WMME_Chapter_9 module, and then create the WMME_Find_Text macro shown here:

```
Sub WMME_Find_Text()

    Selection.HomeKey Unit:=wdStory
    With Selection.Find
        .ClearFormatting
        .Text = "summary"
        .Wrap = wdFindStop
        .Execute
        Do While .Found = True
            If MsgBox("Replace " & Chr(34) & "summary" & Chr(34) _
                & " with " & Chr(34) & "synopsis" & Chr(34) & "?", _
                vbYesNo + vbQuestion, "Replace Text") = vbYes Then
                Selection.TypeText "synopsis"
            Else
                Selection.Collapse direction:=wdCollapseEnd
            End If
            .Execute
        Loop
    End With

End Sub
```

The WMME_Find_Text macro uses a Do While… Loop loop to repeat the search as long as Find finds the search term. Here's what happens:

- The Selection.HomeKey Unit:=wdStory statement moves the insertion point to the beginning of the active document. This is the equivalent of pressing CTRL-HOME when working in Word.

- The With Selection.Find statement begins a With statement that works with the Find object.

■ The .ClearFormatting method clears any formatting set on the Find object.

■ The .Text = "summary" statement sets VBA to look for the word *summary*.

■ The .Wrap = wdFindStop statement sets VBA to stop searching when it reaches the end of the document.

■ The .Execute statement runs the search.

■ If the .Execute statement finds the search term, the Found property of the Find object is True, and so the Do While .Found = True loop runs. This loop displays a Yes/No message box that prompts the user to replace the word "summary" with the word "synopsis." If the user clicks the Yes button, VBA inserts "synopsis" in place of "summary"; if the user clicks the No button, VBA collapses the selection (the found word) to its end so that the search can continue. The .Execute statement in the loop searches for another instance of the search term, and if it finds one, the loop runs again.

With your Report Summary.docx document active, click in the macro, and then press F8 to step through it.

An Example of Replacing a Style

If your job includes fixing documents that other people have formatted, you may find it useful to be able to replace styles in your macros. Click after the WMME_Find_Text macro in your WMME_Chapter_9 module, and then create the WMME_Replace_Style macro shown here:

```
Sub WMME_Replace_Style()

    With ActiveDocument.Content.Find
        .ClearFormatting
        .Text = ""
        .Style = "Heading 4"
```

```
        With .Replacement
            .ClearFormatting
            .Text = ""
            .Style = "Heading 5"
        End With
        .Execute Replace:=wdReplaceAll
    End With

End Sub
```

Here's what happens in the WMME_Replace_Style macro:

- The With ActiveDocument.Content.Find statement makes the macro work with the Find object for the Content object in the ActiveDocument object—that is, with the content of the active document.

- The .ClearFormatting method clears any formatting applied to the Find object.

- The .Text = "" statement sets Find to search for a blank string (no text), so that it will search only for the formatting.

- The .Style = "Heading 4" statement sets the Find object to find the Heading 4 style.

- The With .Replacement statement sets the details of the replacement operation.

- The .ClearFormatting method clears any formatting applied to the Replacement object.

- The .Text = "" statement sets Replace to insert nothing, causing it to apply only the formatting.

- The .Style = "Heading 5" statement sets the Replacement object to apply the Heading 5 style.

151

■ The Execute Replace:=wdReplaceAll statement runs the search and replaces each instance of the Heading 4 style found.

To run this macro, create a new document in Word, type several short paragraphs, and then format them with Heading 4 style. Click in the macro in the Visual Basic Editor, and then press F5 to run the macro. Word changes each Heading 4 paragraph to a Heading 5 paragraph.

Work with Bookmarks

Word's bookmarks—the invisible markers you can insert in a document—can be a great way of having the user fill in particular parts of a document, either working on their own or using one of your macros. By adding bookmarks, you give yourself easy access to the parts of the document you want to manipulate. Even if the user adds or deletes paragraphs in the document, the bookmark stays where you put it—unless the user happens to delete it, either intentionally or by accident. (You can make such accidents less likely by displaying bookmark markers, as discussed later in this chapter.)

Understand What Bookmarks Are and What You Can Do with Them

Word provides two different types of bookmarks:

- Regular bookmarks you create or the user creates

- Secret, hidden bookmarks that Word itself maintains

As you probably know from working in Word, you can use a regular bookmark to mark a point in text, a range in text, or an object. Figure 10-1 shows a document containing three bookmarks, one of each type.

Bookmark marking an image

Figure 10-1 A bookmark can mark a point, a range, or an object such as a picture.

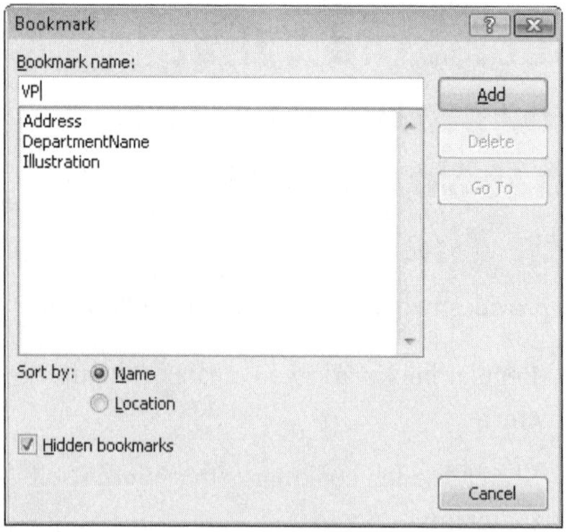

Bookmark marking a range in the document

Our office is located at ⟶ **Bookmark marking a point in the document**

The [Marketing Department] is located on the fifth floor.

To insert a bookmark, place the insertion point or select the object, and then choose Insert | Links | Bookmark. Type the name in the Bookmark dialog box (see Figure 10-2), and then click the Add button.

VBA uses the Bookmark object to represent a bookmark, and gathers all the Bookmark objects for a document into the Bookmarks collection. You access a Bookmark object through the Bookmarks collection, specifying it either by its given name or by its index position in the collection.

Figure 10-2 The Bookmark dialog box lets you create, go to, and delete bookmarks manually.

Get Set Up to Work Through This Chapter

To give yourself space to work with bookmarks, follow these steps to open the Visual Basic Editor and create a new module in which you can create the macros:

1. Open Microsoft Word if it's not already running.

2. Create a new blank document by pressing CTRL-N. (If you just opened Word, and Word created a new document for you, use that document.)

3. Type three or four short paragraphs of text—anything you want—so that you'll have something to work with.

4. Save the document under the name **WMME Bookmarks.docx** in your WMME folder.

5. Press ALT-F11 to open the Visual Basic Editor.

6. If the Visual Basic Editor opens a Code window for a module you worked with recently, click the window's Close button (the × button) to close it.

7. Right-click the Normal template and then choose Insert | Module from the context menu to insert a new module in the Normal template.

8. Press F4 to put the focus in the Properties window.

9. Type **WMME_Chapter_10** as the new name for the module, replacing the default name (such as Module1), and then press ENTER to apply the change.

Work with Regular Bookmarks

Regular bookmarks are those that you insert in a document either manually (using the Bookmark dialog box) or by using VBA. In this section, you'll learn how to create regular bookmarks, go to them, retrieve and change their contents, and also delete them.

MEMO

You can create a hidden bookmark by using an underscore as the first character in the bookmark's name. Creating a hidden bookmark prevents the book-mark from appearing in the Bookmark dialog box unless the user selects the Hidden Bookmarks check box.

Create a Bookmark

To create a bookmark, you use the Add method of the Bookmarks collection. The syntax looks like this:

```
Bookmarks.Add(Name [, Range])
```

Here, *Name* is a required argument giving the name of the bookmark you're adding. The name must start with a letter and can contain up to 40 characters. After that first letter, the rest of the name can be any combination of letters, numbers, and underscores. Spaces aren't allowed.

Range is an optional Variant argument that tells VBA where to insert the bookmark. Normally, you'll want to specify the range; if you don't, VBA inserts the bookmark wherever the selection currently is.

Try this example of creating a bookmark in your WMME Bookmarks.docx document:

```
Sub WMME_Creating_a_Bookmark()
    With Documents("WMME Bookmarks.docx")
        .Bookmarks.Add Name:="Bookmark1", _
            Range:=.Paragraphs(3).Range
    End With
End Sub
```

Find Out Whether a Bookmark Exists

Before you go to or manipulate a bookmark, make sure that it exists—if it doesn't, you'll get an error. To do so, check the Exists property of the Bookmarks collection like this:

```
Sub WMME_Going_to_a_Bookmark()
    With Documents("WMME Bookmarks.docx")
        If .Bookmarks.Exists("Bookmark1") Then
            .Bookmarks("Bookmark1").Select
        End If
    End With
End Sub
```

MEMO

If you run the Add method and specify the name of a book-mark you've already used, VBA overwrites the existing bookmark without warning you.

Go to a Bookmark

To go to a bookmark, use the Select method of the appropriate Bookmark object, as in the previous example:

```
.Bookmarks("Bookmark1").Select
```

You can identify the bookmark either by its name (which is normally most useful) or by its position in the Bookmarks collection. For example, the following statement selects the first bookmark:

```
With Documents("WMME Bookmarks.docx")
    .Bookmarks(1).Select
End With
```

There's a complication here: Word can sort bookmarks either alphabetically by their names or by their positions in the document. So before selecting a bookmark by its index position, set the DefaultSorting property of the Bookmarks collection to wdSortByName or wdSortByLocation first so that you know which you'll get:

```
With Documents("WMME Bookmarks.docx")
    .Bookmarks.DefaultSorting = wdSortByName
    .Bookmarks(1).Select
End With
```

Retrieve the Text Contained in a Bookmark

To retrieve the text contained in a bookmark, return the Text property of the bookmark's range. For example, the following statement displays a message box showing the text in the bookmark named Bookmark1 in the document named WMME Bookmarks.docx:

```
MsgBox Documents("WMME Bookmarks.docx"). _
    Bookmarks("Bookmark1").Range.Text
```

Set the Text in a Bookmark

Getting the text contained in a bookmark is handy, but what you will often need to do is set the contents of a bookmark. You can do this by assigning a string of text to the Text property of the bookmark's range—but when you do so, VBA deletes the bookmark as it changes the text.

To work around this, define a range (as discussed in the previous chapter) and set the range to the bookmark's range. You can then delete the bookmark, set the Text property of the range, and then add a bookmark where the range is. Try creating and stepping through the following macro, which does just that:

```
Sub WMME_Change_Bookmark_Text()

    Dim rngBookmark As Range

    With Documents("WMME Bookmarks.docx")
        Set rngBookmark = .Bookmarks("Bookmark1").Range
        .Bookmarks("Bookmark1").Delete
        rngBookmark.Text = "Here's the new text."
        .Bookmarks.Add Name:="Bookmark1", Range:=rngBookmark
    End With

End Sub
```

Delete a Bookmark with or Without Its Contents

To delete a bookmark but leave its contents intact, use the Delete method of the appropriate Bookmark object. For example, the WMME_Change_ Bookmark_Text macro deletes the bookmark named Bookmark1 in the document named WMME Bookmarks.docx:

```
Documents("WMME Bookmarks.docx").Bookmarks("Bookmark1").Delete
```

REMOVE ALL THE BOOKMARKS FROM A DOCUMENT

If you need to remove all the bookmarks from a document, declare an object of the Bookmark type, and then use a For Each... Next loop to go through the Bookmarks collection. Here's an example:

```
Sub WMME_Delete_All_Bookmarks_in_Document()

    Dim bkBookmark As Bookmark

    For Each bkBookmark In ActiveDocument.Bookmarks
        bkBookmark.Delete
    Next bkBookmark

End Sub
```

MEMO

To turn on the display of bookmark markers when working in Word, click the Microsoft Office button, click Word Options, and then click the Advanced category. Scroll down to the Show Document Content section, select the Show Bookmarks check box, and then click the OK button.

To delete a bookmark and its contents, return the bookmark's range, and then delete it, like this:

```
Documents("WMME Bookmarks.docx")_
    .Bookmarks("Bookmark1").Range.Delete
```

Display Bookmark Markers So That the User Can See the Bookmarks

To prevent users from accidentally deleting the bookmarks on which your macros depend, you can turn on the display of bookmark markers:

```
Documents("WMME Bookmarks.docx").ActiveWindow._
    View.ShowBookmarks = True
```

Set the ShowBookmarks property to False when you want to turn off the display of bookmark markers again.

Make the Most of Word's Secret Bookmarks

Even if you haven't created any bookmarks in your documents, Word maintains a slew of its own secret bookmarks (see Table 10-1). You can access these bookmarks through VBA and put them to good use in your macros.

159

Bookmark Name	Explanation
\Sel	The current selection or (if there is none) the position of the insertion point.
\PrevSel1	The location of the previous edit (where the insertion point goes if you press SHIFT-F5 once when working in Word).
\PrevSel2	The location of the second-previous edit (where the insertion point goes if you press SHIFT-F5 twice when working in Word).
\StartOfSel	The start of the current selection, or the position of the insertion point if the selection is collapsed.
\EndOfSel	The end of the current selection, or the position of the insertion point if the selection is collapsed.
\Line	The first line of the current selection.
\Char	The first character of the current selection, or the character to the right of the insertion point if the selection is collapsed.
\Para	The current paragraph (or the first paragraph in a selection longer than a paragraph).
\Section	The current section (or the first section in a selection that spans two or more sections).
\Doc	The entire contents of the document except for the last paragraph mark (the one that contains the document's formatting).
\Page	The entire contents of the page containing the selection (unless it's the last page in the document, in which case this bookmark doesn't include the last paragraph mark).
\StartOfDoc	The start of the document. This bookmark has no contents, but it's useful for quickly going to the start of the document.
\EndOfDoc	The end of the document.
\Cell	The table cell containing the selection (or the first cell if the selection includes multiple cells).
\Table	The table containing the selection (or the first table if the selection includes multiple tables).
\HeadingLevel	The heading that contains or precedes the selection, including any subheadings below this heading.

Table 10-1   Word's Secret Bookmarks

To try working with Word's secret bookmarks, create this macro, step through it, and watch what happens:

```
Sub WMME_Using_Built_in_Bookmarks()

    With Documents("WMME Bookmarks.docx")
        If Selection.StoryType <> wdMainTextStory Then _
            .Windows(1).View.SeekView = wdSeekMainDocument
        .Bookmarks("\Sel").Copy "CurrentSelection"
        .Bookmarks("\EndOfDoc").Select
        Selection.TypeParagraph
        Selection.TypeText "End of the document."
        .Bookmarks("CurrentSelection").Select
        .Bookmarks("CurrentSelection").Delete
    End With

End Sub
```

MEMO

All the built-in bookmarks are in the main *story* of the document, the part of the document that contains the main text. If the selection is currently in another story, such as the header and footer story or the footnotes story, you must switch to the main story before you can access the built-in bookmarks.

Here's what this macro does:

1. Switches to the main document story if the current selection is in another story. (See the nearby Memo.)

2. Copies the bookmark for the current selection (the built-in \Sel bookmark) to a new bookmark called CurrentSelection.

3. Moves to the end of the document by selecting the built-in \EndOfDoc bookmark.

4. Types a paragraph and some anodyne text.

5. Selects the CurrentSelection bookmark so that the selection is where the user left it.

6. Deletes the CurrentSelection bookmark.

Work with Tables

When you need to lay out complex information in a Word document, you'll often need to use a table. Tables can save you any amount of time over fiddling with tabs; they give you quick access to your text by row, column, or cell; and you can easily apply a wide variety of formatting.

This chapter shows you how to create tables using VBA, both starting a table from scratch and converting existing text to a table—and back again if necessary. You'll also learn how to add and delete rows and columns and format the table and its contents.

Get Set Up to Work Through This Chapter

To give yourself space to work with tables, follow these steps to open the Visual Basic Editor and create a new module in which you can write the macros:

1. Open Microsoft Word if it's not already running. If it is running, close any open documents.

2. Press ALT-F11 to open the Visual Basic Editor.

3. If the Visual Basic Editor opens a Code window for a module you worked with recently, click the window's Close button (the × button) to close it.

4. Right-click the Normal template and then choose Insert | Module from the context menu to insert a new module in the Normal template.

5. Press F4 to put the focus in the Properties window.

6. Type **WMME_Chapter_11** as the new name for the module, replacing the default name (such as Module1), and then press ENTER to apply the change.

7. Press CTRL-G to open the Immediate window. You'll remember that this window lets you execute single commands without having to put them in a macro.

8. If no document is open in Word, type **documents.add** and press ENTER to create a new document based on the Normal template. You'll add the tables to this document. (If you opened Word in step 1, and Word created a blank document for you, use that document instead.)

9. In Word, save the document under the name **WMME Tables.docx** in your WMME folder.

You're now ready to start working through this chapter.

Create a Table from Scratch

First, let's create a table from scratch. To do so, you use the Add method of the Tables collection. The syntax looks like this:

```
Document.Tables.Add Range, NumRows, NumColumns,
DefaultTableBehavior, AutoFitBehavior
```

All of this is pretty straightforward:

- *Document* is the document with which you're working—for example, ActiveDocument for the active document, or a Document object by name, such as Documents("WMME Tables.docx").

■ *Range* is the range in which you want to add the table. If you have a selection, you can specify the range in relation to it; for example, you can simply use Range:=Selection.Range to use the range the user has selected. If you do not have a selection, you specify the document and the part of the document—for example, at the first paragraph in the document.

■ *NumRows* is a required Long argument that controls the number of rows in the table.

■ *NumColumns* is a required Long argument that controls the number of columns in the table.

■ *DefaultTableBehavior* is an optional Variant argument that tells VBA whether to resize the columns to fit their contents (wdWord9TableBehavior) or not (wdWord8TableBehavior).

■ *AutoFitBehavior* is an optional Variant argument that you use when you've set *DefaultTableBehavior* to wdWord9TableBehavior. This argument tells VBA whether to resize the columns in the table to accommodate their contents (wdAutoFitContent), to autofit the table to the document window (wdAutoFitWindow), or to use fixed column widths (wdAutoFitFixed).

Try this example of adding a table:

1. Click in the Code window for the WMME_Chapter_11 module and create the stub of a macro:

```
Sub WMME_Add_a_Table()

End Sub
```

2. Add the following statement, using VBA's code-completion features to enter the constants for DefaultTableBehavior and AutoFitBehavior:

```
Documents("WMME Tables.docx").Tables.Add _
    Range:=Selection.Range, _
```

```
                    NumRows:=4, NumColumns:=5, _
                    DefaultTableBehavior:=wdWord9TableBehavior, _
                    AutoFitBehavior:=wdAutoFitContent
```

3. Press F5 or click the Run Sub/UserForm button to run the macro.
   VBA inserts a table with five columns and four rows at the position
   of the selection in the first open document. VBA autofits the column
   width to the contents, so, because the cells have no content, the
   columns are absurdly narrow. That'll change when you add content
   to the cells.

Add Content to a Table's Cells

You can add text to a cell by assigning a string to the Text property of the
appropriate Cell object. You can reach the cell in any of these ways:

- **By its position in the table**   Tables(1).Cells(1, 2) tells VBA to use the
  cell in the first row (the 1) and the second column (the 2). This is
  usually the easiest way to reference cells.

- **By its position in a row**   Tables(1).Rows(1).Cells(2) tells VBA to use
  the second cell in the first row. You can't reference by row when you've
  merged cells from two or more rows.

- **By its position in a column**   Tables(1).Columns(3).Cells(4) tells VBA
  to use the fourth cell in the third column. You can't reference by
  column when you've merged cells from two or more columns.

Follow these steps to create a macro that adds content to the table:

1. After the WMME_Add_a_Table macro in your WMME_Chapter_11
   module, create a new macro named WMME_Add_Contents_to_Table:

```
Sub WMME_Add_Contents_to_Table()

End Sub
```

2. Start a With statement that works with the first Table object in the WMME Tables.docx document:

```
With Documents("WMME Tables.docx").Tables(1)
```

3. Use the Cell object in the Table object to insert contents in the five cells of the first row:

```
.Cell(1, 1).Range.Text = "Item"
.Cell(1, 2).Range.Text = "Kept in Room"
.Cell(1, 3).Range.Text = "Brand"
.Cell(1, 4).Range.Text = "Description"
.Cell(1, 5).Range.Text = "Value ($)"
```

4. Go through the five columns in the Columns collection to insert contents in the cells in the second row:

```
.Columns(1).Cells(2).Range.Text = "Digital camera"
.Columns(2).Cells(2).Range.Text = "Study"
.Columns(3).Cells(2).Range.Text = "Fujitsu"
.Columns(4).Cells(2).Range.Text = "FR77 model"
.Columns(5).Cells(2).Range.Text = "100"
```

5. Create a With statement that goes through the Rows collection to insert contents in the cells in the third row:

```
With .Rows(3)
    .Cells(1).Range.Text = "PC"
    .Cells(2).Range.Text = "Study"
    .Cells(3).Range.Text = "Dell"
    .Cells(4).Range.Text = "Studio Desktop"
    .Cells(5).Range.Text = "300"
End With
```

6. End the With statement for the Document object:

```
End With
```

Here's the complete macro. Arrange the Word window and the Visual Basic Editor so that you can see both. Press F8 to step through the code, and watch the columns change width as the contents appear in the cells.

```
Sub WMME_Add_Contents_to_Table()
    With Documents("WMME Tables.docx").Tables(1)
        .Cell(1, 1).Range.Text = "Item"
        .Cell(1, 2).Range.Text = "Kept in Room"
        .Cell(1, 3).Range.Text = "Brand"
        .Cell(1, 4).Range.Text = "Description"
        .Cell(1, 5).Range.Text = "Value ($)"
        .Columns(1).Cells(2).Range.Text = "Digital camera"
        .Columns(2).Cells(2).Range.Text = "Study"
        .Columns(3).Cells(2).Range.Text = "Fujitsu"
        .Columns(4).Cells(2).Range.Text = "FR77 model"
        .Columns(5).Cells(2).Range.Text = "100"
        With .Rows(3)
            .Cells(1).Range.Text = "PC"
            .Cells(2).Range.Text = "Study"
            .Cells(3).Range.Text = "Dell"
            .Cells(4).Range.Text = "Studio Desktop"
            .Cells(5).Range.Text = "300"
        End With
    End With
End Sub
```

Convert a Table to Text

Now try converting your table to text so that you'll have text suitable for converting into a table. To convert a table to text, you use the ConvertToText method, which uses this syntax:

```
Table.ConvertToText(Separator, NestedTables)
```

Here's what the arguments mean:

- *Separator* is an optional Variant argument that tells VBA which separator character to use: tabs (wdSeparateByTabs; the default if you don't specify the argument), paragraphs (wdSeparateByParagraphs), commas (wdSeparateByCommas), or the default list separator (wdSeparateByDefaultListSeparator).

- *NestedTables* is an optional Variant argument that applies only when you're separating by paragraphs. You can set this argument to False to prevent Word from converting nested tables. If you omit this argument, or set it to True, Word converts the nested tables.

Create this single-statement macro, and then press F5 to run it:

```
Sub WMME_Convert_Table_to_Text()
    Documents("WMME Tables.docx").Tables(1) _
        .ConvertToText Separator:=wdSeparateByTabs
End Sub
```

Word converts the table to paragraphs of text, separating the contents of each column with tabs.

Convert Existing Text to a Table

Now that you've reduced your table to text, convert it straight back to a table by using the ConvertToTable method. Here's the syntax:

```
Range.ConvertToTable(Separator, NumRows, NumColumns,_
    InitialColumnWidth, Format, ApplyBorders,_
    ApplyShading, ApplyFont, ApplyColor, ApplyHeadingRows,_
    ApplyLastRow, ApplyFirstColumn, ApplyLastColumn,_
    AutoFit, AutoFitBehavior, DefaultTableBehavior)
```

169

> **MEMO**
>
> Always specify the separator when converting text to a table. If you don't, VBA uses the default list separator, the hyphen, which is seldom helpful or amusing.

> **MEMO**
>
> If you use the Format argument to apply an autoformat, you can set the *ApplyBorders*, *ApplyShading*, *ApplyFont*, *ApplyColor*, *ApplyHeadingRows*, *ApplyLastRow*, *ApplyFirstColumn*, and *ApplyLastColumn* arguments to True to apply those parts of the autoformat you want. For example, to apply whatever heading row formatting the autoformat uses, enter ApplyHeadingRows :=True.

As you can see, the ConvertToTable method has a slew of arguments. Here are the most useful ones:

- *Separator* is an optional Variant argument that tells VBA where to split the columns. You can use the same separators as for converting a table to text (wdSeparateByTabs, wdSeparateByParagraphs, wdSeparateByCommas, or wdSeparateByDefaultListSeparator) or specify your own separator by using Separator:="" (with the character between the quotes).

- *NumRows* is an optional Variant argument that you can set to tell VBA how many rows the table should have.

- *NumColumns* is an optional Variant argument that you can set to tell VBA how many columns the table should have. If the separator characters are all present and correct, you don't need to specify *NumRows* or *NumColumns*.

- *InitialColumnWidth* is an optional Variant argument that you can set to give the initial column width in points. Omit this argument to have VBA set the column width automatically.

- *Format* is an optional Variant argument that you can set to apply an autoformat such as wdTableFormat3DEffects1 or the mendaciously named wdTableFormatElegant. Look up the WdTableFormat enumeration in the Object Browser to see the full list of formats.

- *AutoFit* is an optional Variant argument that you can set to True to make Word automatically adjust the column widths to suit their contents.

- *AutoFitBehavior* is an optional Variant argument that you use when you've set *DefaultTableBehavior* to wdWord9TableBehavior. This argument tells VBA whether to resize the columns in the table to accommodate their contents (wdAutoFitContent), to autofit the table to the document window (wdAutoFitWindow), or to use fixed column widths (wdAutoFitFixed).

■ *DefaultTableBehavior* is an optional Variant argument that tells VBA whether to resize the columns to fit their contents (wdWord9TableBehavior) or not (wdWord8TableBehavior).

After all that preamble, converting text to a table may be disappointing. Nevertheless, try creating the WMME_Convert_Text_to_Table macro shown here:

```
Sub WMME_Convert_Text_to_Table()
    Selection.ConvertToTable Separator:=wdSeparateByTabs, _
        AutoFit:=True, _
        AutoFitBehavior:=wdAutoFitWindow, _
        DefaultTableBehavior:=wdWord9TableBehavior
End Sub
```

In the WMME Tables.docx document, select the first three paragraphs of the text produced when you converted the table. Then click in the Visual Basic Editor and press F5 to run this macro and convert the text back to a table.

Add a Column or Row to a Table

To add a column to a table, use the Add method of the Columns collection. The syntax is simple:

```
Columns.Add BeforeColumn
```

Here, *BeforeColumn* is an optional Variant argument that specifies the column before which to add the new column. If you omit this argument, VBA inserts the column after the last column, which is usually the least harmful place to put it.

Similarly, you use the Add method of the Rows collection to add a row to a table. The syntax is

```
Rows.Add BeforeRow
```

As you've probably guessed, *BeforeRow* is an optional Variant argument that specifies the row before which to add the new row. If you omit this argument, VBA inserts the row after the last row.

171

Try creating and running this short macro to add a new column before the second column and to add two new rows at the end of the table:

```
Sub WMME_Insert_a_Column_and_a_Row()
    With Documents("WMME Tables.docx").Tables(1)
        .Columns.Add BeforeColumn:=.Columns(2)
        .Rows.Add
        .Rows.Add
    End With
End Sub
```

Delete a Column or Row

To delete a column, you use the Delete method with the appropriate Column object. Similarly, to delete a row, you use the Delete method with the appropriate Row object.

Try creating and stepping through this short macro to delete the column and the rows you just added to the table:

```
Sub WMME_Delete_Rows_and_Column()
    With Documents("WMME Tables.docx").Tables(1)
        .Columns(2).Delete
        .Rows(4).Delete
        .Rows(4).Delete
    End With
End Sub
```

Notice that the macro deletes the fourth row twice. As you'll see when you step through the macro, after the first time the macro deletes the fourth row, the fifth row becomes the fourth, so the macro can delete the same-numbered row again. Alternatively, you could delete the fifth row and then the fourth—but deleting the fourth row and then deleting the fifth would cause an error, because the fifth row would no longer be there.

DELETING AN ENTIRE TABLE

To delete an entire table, simply use the Delete method on the appropriate Table object. For example, the following statement deletes the first table in the active document:

```
ActiveDocument.Tables(1).Delete
```

Format a Table

As you'll know from working interactively, Word lets you format tables in a wide variety of ways. This section gets you started with table formatting and then encourages you to explore further formatting on your own as needed.

Set the Preferred Width of a Table

To set the preferred width of a table, you first set the PreferredWidthType property to tell VBA which width measurement you're using:

WdPreferredWidthType	Explanation
wdPreferredWidthAuto	VBA sets the table width automatically.
wdPreferredWidthPercent	You specify the table width as a percentage of the window width.
wdPreferredWidthPoints	You specify the table width as a number of points.

Once you've set the PreferredWidthType property, you can set the PreferredWidth property to the appropriate percentage or number of points. For example, you can use the following macro to set the preferred width to 90 percent of the window's width:

```
Sub WMME_Set_Table_Preferred_Width()
    With Documents("WMME Tables.docx").Tables(1)
        .PreferredWidthType = wdPreferredWidthPercent
        .PreferredWidth = 90
    End With
End Sub
```

Set Column Width and Row Height

To set the width of a column, you specify the column and the measurement in points for its Width property. Similarly, to set the height of a row, you specify the row and the measurement in points for its Height property.

Try this example to change the width of the first column and the height of the first row:

```
Sub WMME_Set_Column_Width_and_Row_Height()
    With Documents("WMME Tables.docx").Tables(1)
        .Columns(1).Width = 100
        .Rows(1).Height = 50
    End With
End Sub
```

Apply Font Formatting to the Table

To apply font formatting to a table, simply identify the part of the table you want to format, and then specify the font formatting. Try this example to format the heading row of your table:

```
Sub WMME_Apply_Font_Formatting_to_Table_Heading_Rows()
    With Documents("WMME Tables.docx")_
        .Tables(1).Rows(1).Range.Font
        .Name = "Arial"
        .Size = 14
        .Bold = True
        .Color = wdColorDarkBlue
        .SmallCaps = True
    End With
End Sub
```

Work with Documents and Folders

In this chapter, you'll learn how to create and save new documents and templates, open and close documents, and create and delete files and folders. You'll also learn how to manipulate document windows and change the view.

Get Set Up to Work Through This Chapter

Follow these steps to open the Visual Basic Editor and create a new module that you'll use for working with documents:

1. Open Microsoft Word if it's not already running. If it is running, close any open documents.

2. Press ALT-F11 to open the Visual Basic Editor.

3. If the Visual Basic Editor opens a Code window for a module you worked with recently, click the window's Close button (the × button) to close it.

4. Right-click the Normal template and then choose Insert | Module from the context menu to insert a new module in the Normal template.

5. Press F4 to put the focus in the Properties window.

6. Type **WMME_Chapter_12** as the new name for the module, replacing the default name (such as Module1), and then press ENTER to apply the change.

Create New Documents

To create a new document, use the Add method of the Documents collection. The syntax looks like this:

```
Documents.Add Template, NewTemplate, DocumentType, Visible
```

Here's what the syntax means:

- *Template* is an optional Variant argument that you use to base the new document on a particular template. If you omit this argument, Word bases the new document on the Normal template.

- *NewTemplate* is an optional Variant argument that you set to True if you want to create a new template rather than a new document. When creating a new document, you can either omit this argument or set it to False to make your code completely explicit.

- *DocumentType* is an optional Variant argument that lets you create different types of document. Use wdNewBlankDocument (or omit the argument) when you want a regular document, wdNewEmailMessage for a new e-mail message, wdNewFrameset for a frameset (for web pages), wdNewWebPage for a web page, or wdNewXMLDocument for an XML document.

- *Visible* is an optional Variant argument that lets you control whether the new document is visible. Set this argument to False to hide the document or to True (or omit the argument) to show the document as usual.

Because all these arguments are optional, you can create a new blank document (and make it visible) by omitting all the arguments:

```
Sub WMME_Create_a_Blank_Document()
    Documents.Add
End Sub
```

Run this, and you'll get a new document called Document1 (or the next unused name, such as Document2).

Try this example of creating a new document based on a template. If you don't have the EquityFax.dotx template, use a template you do have instead.

```
Sub WMME_Create_a_Document()
    Documents.Add Template:= _
        "C:\Program Files\Microsoft Office\Templates\1033\
FAX\EquityFax.dotx", _
            NewTemplate:=False
End Sub
```

Next, copy the WMME_Create_a_Document macro you just created, paste it, and adapt it as follows so that it creates a new template based on the template you just used:

```
Sub WMME_Create_a_Template()
    Documents.Add Template:= _
        "C:\Program Files\Microsoft Office\Templates\1033\
FAX\EquityFax.dotx", _
            NewTemplate:=True
End Sub
```

When you run this, you'll get a template named Template1 (or the next unused name).

MEMO

If you don't specify the path to the template, Word assumes you're using the default template folder.

177

FIND WORD'S TEMPLATE FOLDERS

If you need to find out where the current user templates folder or the workgroup templates folder is, check the DefaultFilePath property of the Options object with the wdUserTemplatesPath constant or the wdWorkgroupTemplatesPath constant, respectively.

Word automatically sets the user templates path to the folder in which it installs the templates for the user, but the workgroup templates path may be blank unless an administrator has set it. (For example, an administrator may have pointed the workgroup templates path to a network folder.)

For example, the following statement displays the user templates path in a message box:

```
MsgBox Options.DefaultFilePath
(wdUserTemplatesPath)
```

The following statement sets the workgroup templates path to a network folder:

```
Options.DefaultFilePath(wdWorkgroup
TemplatesPath) = "Z:\Users\Shared\
Templates"
```

MEMO

If you want to create a document and prompt the user to save it, you can simply use **Documents .Add.Save**.

Save Documents

Sometimes you may want to create a document, use it as scratch space to work in, and then close it without saving it ever—but more often, you'll need to save your documents. To save a document for the first time, you use the SaveAs method of the appropriate Document object. After that, you can simply use the Save method.

Save a Document for the First Time

Here's the syntax for the SaveAs method:

```
Document.SaveAs(FileName, FileFormat, LockComments, Password,_
    AddToRecentFiles, WritePassword, ReadOnlyRecommended,_
    EmbedTrueTypeFonts, SaveNativePictureFormat, SaveFormsData,_
    SaveAsAOCELetter, Encoding, InsertLineBreaks,_
    AllowSubstitutions, LineEnding, AddBiDiMarks)
```

MEMO

When saving a document, you'll almost always want to specify the *FileName* argument; if you don't, Word uses the current folder (whichever that may be; see the nearby sidebar) and a shortened version of the document's default name (for example, Doc10.docx).

As you can see, there are a ton of arguments. Here, we'll look at only the first five arguments, which are the ones you'll need most of the time:

- *FileName* is an optional Variant argument giving the name and folder path under which to save the document.

- *FileFormat* is an optional Variant argument telling Word which file format to save the document in. These are the WdSaveFormat constants you'll find most useful:

WdSaveFormat Constant	Explanation
wdFormatXMLDocument	Word 2007 Document format (no macros)
wdFormatDocument	Word 97–2003 Document format
wdFormatXMLDocumentMacroEnabled	Word 2007 Macro-Enabled Document format
wdFormatXMLTemplate	Word 2007 Template format (no macros)
wdFormatXMLTemplateMacroEnabled	Word 2007 Macro-Enabled Template format
wdFormatTemplate	Word 97–2003 Template format

- *LockComments* is an optional Variant argument that you can set to True to lock the document so that anyone who opens it can only add comments. If you omit this argument, VBA sets LockComments to False, leaving the document open for edits.

- *Password* is an optional Variant argument that you can use to set the password required to open the document. Don't put the password itself in your code, or anyone will be able to read it; instead, use an input box to prompt the user for the password, and then apply the password in your code.

You can also use the SaveAs method to save an already-saved document under a different name or in a different folder (or both).

■ *AddToRecentFiles* is an optional Variant argument that you can set to False to prevent Word from adding the document to the Recent Documents list on the Microsoft Office button menu. If you omit this argument or set it to True, Word adds the file to the list.

For example, create the following macro, click one of the unsaved documents you've created (not a template), and then run the macro to save the document. As usual, change the file path to suit your setup.

```
Sub WMME_Save_a_Document()
    ActiveDocument.SaveAs FileName:=_
        "C:\Users\Dan\Documents\WMME\Sample Document.docx", _
        FileFormat:=wdFormatXMLDocument
End Sub
```

Save a Document That Already Has a Filename

Once you've saved a document with a name (and folder, and file format), you can save it again easily by using the Save method, just as you would save the document by pressing CTRL-S or clicking the Save button when working interactively. The Save method needs no arguments, so you use it like this:

```
ActiveDocument.Save
```

Leave all these documents and templates open for the moment. You'll close them next.

Close Documents

To close a document, use the Close method of the appropriate Document object. The syntax looks like this:

```
Document.Close(SaveChanges, OriginalFormat, RouteDocument)
```

Here's what the three arguments mean:

- *SaveChanges* is an optional Variant argument that you can use to save changes automatically (wdSaveChanges), discard the changes (wdDoNotSaveChanges), or prompt the user to decide (wdPromptToSaveChanges).

- *OriginalFormat* is an optional Variant argument that lets you control which format Word uses for saving unsaved changes. Use wdOriginalDocumentFormat to use the same format, wdWordDocument to use the Word 2007 Document format, or wdPromptUser to have Word prompt the user to pick a format.

- *RouteDocument* is an optional Variant argument that you set to True if you need to route a document with a routing slip attached.

For example, close the document you just saved by creating and running this macro:

```
Sub WMME_Close_a_Document()
    Documents("Sample Document.docx").Close _
        SaveChanges:=wdPromptToSaveChanges
End Sub
```

Unless you made any changes since you saved it, Word will simply close the document without prompting you to save changes.

Try making Word prompt you to save changes. Click in your unsaved template, type a few characters, and then return to the Visual Basic Editor. Press CTRL-G to open the Immediate window, type the following statement, and then press ENTER to execute it:

```
ActiveDocument.Close SaveChanges:=wdPromptToSaveChanges
```

This time, Word prompts you to save the changes. Click the No button.

Lastly, create a couple more unsaved documents in Word (press CTRL-N a couple of times), and then close all your open documents by using the Close

181

method of the Documents collection. Click in the Immediate window, type the following statement, and then press ENTER:

```
Documents.Close SaveChanges:=wdDoNotSaveChanges
```

Open Documents

To open a document via VBA, you use the Open method of the appropriate Document object in the Documents collection.

Here's the syntax for the Open method:

```
Documents.Open(FileName, ConfirmConversions, ReadOnly,_
    AddToRecentFiles, PasswordDocument, PasswordTemplate,_
    Revert, WritePasswordDocument, WritePasswordTemplate,_
    Format, Encoding, Visible, OpenConflictDocument,_
    OpenAndRepair, DocumentDirection, NoEncodingDialog)
```

Usually, you'll need only the first four arguments, so I'll explain those and leave you to investigate the others at your leisure. Here are the important arguments:

- *FileName* is a required Variant argument that gives the name (usually preceded by the folder path) of the document.

- *ConfirmConversions* is an optional Variant argument that you can set to True to force VBA to display the Convert File dialog box if the document isn't in Word format. If you're opening a Word document, you don't need to bother with this argument.

- *ReadOnly* is an optional Variant argument that you can set to True to open the document in read-only format. Read-only format prevents the user from saving changes to the document under the same name and folder. This is occasionally useful.

- *AddToRecentFiles* is an optional Variant argument that you can set to False to prevent Word from adding the document to the Recent Documents list on the Microsoft Office button menu. This lets you open documents in your macros without messing up the user's Recent Documents list. If you set this argument to True or omit it, Word adds the document to the list as usual.

For example, try opening your Report Summary.docx document from the WMME folder without adding it to the Recent Documents list. Create this macro, substituting your folder path:

```
Sub WMME_Open_a_Document()
    Documents.Open FileName:= _
        "C:\Users\Petra\Documents\WMME\Report Summary.docx", _
        AddToRecentFiles:=False
End Sub
```

Run the macro to open the document. In Word, open the Microsoft Office button menu and verify that Report Summary.docx doesn't appear at the top (unless you just opened it normally yourself before running this macro, of course).

183

CHANGE THE CURRENT FOLDER OR THE CURRENT DRIVE

In your macros, you may need to change the current folder or drive so that when the user tries to open or save a document, the dialog box shows the right folder.

To find out what the current folder is, use the CurDir statement (CurDir is short for "current directory"). For example, the following statement displays a message box showing the current folder:

```
MsgBox CurDir
```

Once you know what the current directory is, you can use the ChDir statement to change the current

directory on a drive. For example, the following statement changes the directory to the WMME folder inside the Documents folder on a standard Windows Vista file system:

```
ChDir "C:\Users\Donna\Documents\WMME"
```

Use the ChDrive statement to change the drive. For example, the following statement changes to the Z: drive:

```
ChDrive "Z"
```

Delete a Document

You can delete a document by using a Kill statement and the document's path and filename. You need to make sure that the document is closed when you try to delete it—if it's open, you'll get a "Permission denied" error, which basically means "Word says no."

For example, close your Sample Document.docx document manually, type the following statement in the Immediate window, and then press ENTER to run it:

```
Kill "C:\Users\Dave\Documents\WMME\Sample Document.docx"
```

If the Kill operation is successful, VBA gives you no feedback—but the document is permanently gone.

Create and Delete Folders

Creating and deleting documents (or templates) is well and good, but sometimes you may also need to create or delete folders in your macros.

Create a Folder

To create a folder with VBA, use the MkDir statement (short for "make directory"). This requires only one argument, giving the drive (optionally) and the folder path. For example, the following statement creates a folder named Code within the WMME folder in the Documents folder on a standard Windows Vista file system:

```
MkDir "C:\Users\Dave\Documents\WMME\Code"
```

Delete a Folder

Deleting a folder with VBA is more complex. The statement you need is RmDir (short for "remove directory"). Like MkDir, RmDir needs only one argument, giving the drive (optionally, but preferably) and the folder path.

First, though, you must make sure that the folder has no contents. If the folder contains one or more files, or one or more folders, or both, RmDir gives a Path/File access error.

To delete all files in the folder, you can use a Kill statement with the *.* wildcards. For example, the following statement deletes all the files in the C:\Users\Dave\Documents\WMME\Code folder:

```
Kill "C:\Users\Dave\Documents\WMME\Code\*.*"
```

To remove a folder within the folder, use a RmDir statement with its name. Once the folder is empty, you can use RmDir to remove it—for example:

```
RmDir "C:\Users\Dave\Documents\WMME\Code"
```

Work with Document Windows

Normally, when you open a document, Word shows it to you in a single window. You can manipulate this window by using the first Window object for the Document object. You can also add further windows, as you'll do here. Follow these steps:

1. Run the WMME_Open_a_Document macro to open the Report Summary.docx document again.

2. Start a new macro named WMME_Open_and_Resize_Window:

   ```
   Sub WMME_Open_and_Resize_Window()

   End Sub
   ```

3. Declare an object variable named winMyWindow as being of the Window type:

   ```
   Dim winMyWindow As Window
   ```

4. Set the winMyWindow object variable to represent a new window you open on the Report Summary.docx document by using the Add method:

```
Set winMyWindow = _
    Documents("Report Summary.docx").Windows.Add
```

5. Start a With statement that works with winMyWindow:

```
With winMyWindow
```

6. Position the window by setting its Left property (which controls where the left edge appears) and its Top property (which controls where the top edge appears) to suitable values (in pixels):

```
.Left = 200
.Top = 0
```

7. Resize the window by setting its Height property and its Width property (again, these measurements are in pixels):

```
.Height = 800
.Width = 600
```

8. Set the view to Print Layout view by setting the Type property of the View object in the Window object:

```
.View.Type = wdPrintView
```

9. Set the zoom on the window by setting the PageFit property of the Zoom object in the View object in the Window object:

```
.View.Zoom.PageFit = wdPageFitTextFit
```

10. End the With statement:

```
End With
```

Here's the complete macro. Step through it, and watch what happens.

```
Sub WMME_Open_and_Resize_Window()
    Dim winMyWindow As Window
    Set winMyWindow = _
        Documents("Report Summary.docx").Windows.Add
```

```
      With winMyWindow
          .Left = 200
          .Top = 0
          .Height = 800
          .Width = 600
          .View.Type = wdPrintView
          .View.Zoom.PageFit = wdPageFitTextFit
      End With
End Sub
```

To close the extra window, use the Close method. Press CTRL-G to open the Immediate window, type the following statement, and then press ENTER to run it:

```
Documents("Report Summary.docx").Windows(2).Close
```

Debug Your Macros and Handle Errors

In the best of all possible worlds, your investments will only go up, you'll enjoy rude good health, and your relationships and your code will simply work without problems.

Sooner or later, though, you'll run into errors in your code—or the people who use your macros will. Such errors can be as simple as the user having selected the wrong type of object before running a macro, not having the right type of document open, or not having a document open at all. Or the errors can involve tracking your code through labyrinthine loops of logic to find a tiny mistake that's throwing a wrench in the entire works.

In this chapter, you'll learn how to use VBA's tools for debugging your macros and how to create an error handler that enables your code to deal "gracefully" with errors that occur.

For health, relationship, and investment advice, look elsewhere.

Get Set Up to Work Through This Chapter

To get ready to work through this chapter, follow these steps to open the Visual Basic Editor, create a new module, and create and save a new document:

1. Open Microsoft Word if it's not already running. If it is running, close any open documents.

2. Press ALT-F11 to open the Visual Basic Editor.

3. If the Visual Basic Editor opens a Code window for a module you worked with recently, click the window's Close button (the × button) to close it.

4. Right-click the Normal template and then choose Insert | Module from the context menu to insert a new module in the Normal template.

5. Press F4 to put the focus in the Properties window.

6. Type **WMME_Chapter_13** as the new name for the module, replacing the default name (such as Module1), and then press ENTER to apply the change.

You're now ready to start working through this chapter.

Debug a Macro

Debugging is the process of removing errors ("bugs") from your macros. In this section, you'll meet the tools that the Visual Basic Editor provides to help root out the bugs in your code. First, though, it's helpful to understand which types of errors you are likely to create in your macros.

MEMO

Identify the Four Main Types of Errors

As long as you have the Auto Syntax Check feature turned on (select the Auto Syntax Check check box on the Editor tab in the Options dialog box), VBA manages to catch many compile errors when you move the insertion point to a different statement. Others, like the example here, pop up only when you go to run the code and VBA must compile the whole macro.

The bad news is that you'll typically create four main types of errors in your code. The good news is that VBA helps you eliminate three of them.

- **Language error (syntax error)**   These errors occur when you make a mistake by typing the wrong character or term in the Visual Basic Editor. VBA's automatic-completion features and List Properties/Methods feature help keep language errors to a minimum.

- **Compile error**   These errors occur when you create a statement that VBA can't compile correctly. For example, if you type **ActiveDocument.Close SaveChanges:=wdDontSaveChanges** instead of **ActiveDocument.Close SaveChanges:=wdDoNotSaveChanges**, VBA gives a "Variable not defined" compile error (shown here) when you try to run the code.

- **Runtime error**   These errors occur when you run your code and VBA finds something that doesn't work. For example, if you tell VBA to close a document that isn't open, you'll get the "Bad file name" error message shown in Figure 13-1. Here, the code is fine, and it compiles perfectly—but it won't run because the conditions are wrong.

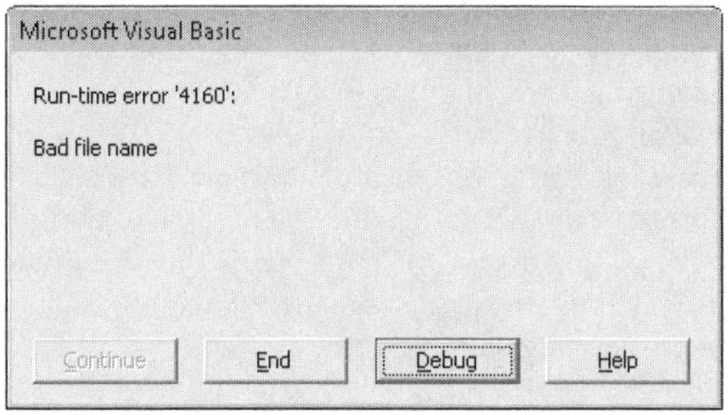

191

Figure 13-1   The "Bad file name" runtime error message occurs when you tell VBA to close a document that isn't open—or when you use a filename that contains characters the file system can't handle.

When you click the Debug button, VBA displays and highlights the offending line of code so that you can fix it.

■ **Program logic error**   These errors occur when your code compiles correctly, runs correctly, and produces the wrong result, such as formatting the wrong document. As far as VBA is concerned, there's no problem, so you're on your own fixing program logic errors.

Meet the Debug Toolbar

The easiest way to access most of the commands and tools you'll be using in the rest of this section is by clicking the buttons on the Debug toolbar (see Figure 13-2). If this toolbar isn't displayed, you can display it by right-clicking

Figure 13-2   The Debug toolbar includes buttons for stepping into, stepping over, and stepping out of a macro.

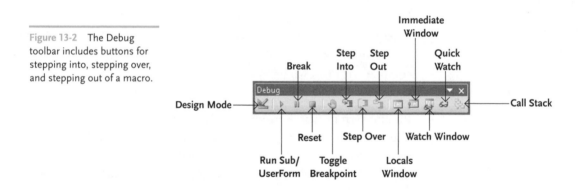

WHEN IS THE BEST TIME TO DEBUG YOUR MACROS?

This is a trick question, because there's no best time to debug your macros. Instead, debugging tends to be an ongoing process that starts when you first try to write the macro and doesn't necessarily end when you distribute the macro to other users.

When you find that a macro you're writing doesn't run the way you intended it to, you're debugging it. At this point, you can iron out the grosser bugs by

trying different approaches in your code until you get it working.

When you try the macro on other users, you'll probably find that they devise alternative ways of running the macro that produce new and exciting bugs. You'll then need to rework the macro, or add error-handling code to it, to take care of these errors.

any displayed toolbar (or the menu bar) and choosing Debug from the context menu (placing a check mark next to Debug).

Step Through Code and Use Breakpoints

Throughout this book, you've been using the Step Into command to go through a macro one statement at a time so that you can see exactly what each statement does. But going statement-by-statement through a long macro can take forever, so VBA provides you with several tools for getting through your code faster while still focusing on the sections that need attention.

Set a Breakpoint to Enter Break Mode

The first tool you can use is the breakpoint. A *breakpoint* is a mark you place on a statement to tell VBA you want to start using Break mode at that point. The Visual Basic Editor doesn't save breakpoints in your code when you close the project, so if you need them the next time you open your project, you have to place them again.

The easiest way to set a breakpoint is to click in the vertical bar at the left side of the Code window next to the statement on which you want to set the breakpoint (see Figure 13-3). The Visual Basic Editor puts a hefty brown dot in the vertical bar and applies a liverish highlight to the statement, making the breakpoint stick out rather more than a sore thumb. Click the dot when you want to remove the breakpoint.

MEMO

You can also set or remove a breakpoint by clicking in the statement and then clicking the Toggle Breakpoint button on the Debug toolbar, or by right-clicking in the statement and then choosing Toggle | Breakpoint from the context menu.

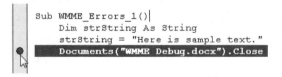

```
Sub WMME_Errors_1()
    Dim strString As String
    strString = "Here is sample text."
    Documents("WMME Debug.docx").Close
```

Figure 13-3   You can set a breakpoint by clicking in the vertical bar at the left side of the Code window.

You can then run the macro by pressing F5 or clicking the Run Sub/UserForm button. When VBA hits the breakpoint, it switches to Break mode, and you can press F8 to execute commands one at a time.

Once you're in Break mode, the Visual Basic Editor makes the Step Out command and the Step Over command available so that you can use them.

Step Out of a Macro

Once you've gotten through the statements you wanted to focus on, you can click the Step Out button on the Debug toolbar (or press CTRL-SHIFT-F8) to proceed through the rest of the macro at full pace.

Step Over a Macro or Function

When the macro you're running calls another macro or a function that you know works fine, you can use the Step Over command to go through that macro or function at full speed and then return to Break mode when execution returns to the current macro.

To step over a macro or function, click the Step Over button on the Debug toolbar or press SHIFT-F8.

Use the Locals Window to Track Variable Values

When a macro consistently produces unexpected results, you can use the Locals window to keep an eye on the variables the macro is using and the values assigned to them. You used the Locals window in Chapter 7 to find out what data type a particular piece of data had.

The easiest way to open the Locals window is to click the Locals Window button on the Debug toolbar. If you prefer, you can choose View | Locals.

While you step through your code, watch the values change (see Figure 13-4), and note any unexpected values. If you've declared any variables without specifying their type, watch to see if the type changes from one Variant subtype to another.

When you've finished using the Locals window, click the Close button (the × button) to close it.

Use the Watch Window to Track Important Values

Being able to view variable values in the Locals window is handy, but sometimes you may need to keep a closer watch on the values of just some

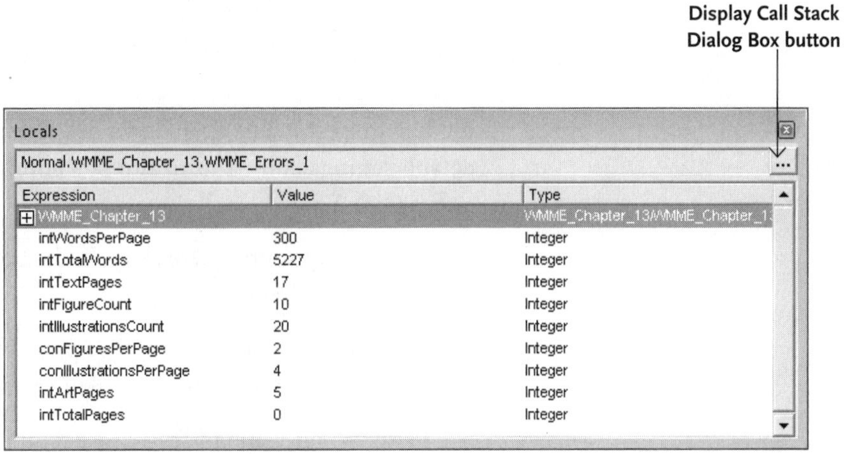

Display Call Stack
Dialog Box button

Figure 13-4   The Locals
window lets you keep an eye
on the value of the variables,
constants, and expressions in
the macro you're running.

Locals

Normal.WMME_Chapter_13.WMME_Errors_1

Expression	Value	Type
WMME_Chapter_13		WMME_Chapter_13\WMME_Chapter_1
intWordsPerPage	300	Integer
intTotalWords	5227	Integer
intTextPages	17	Integer
intFigureCount	10	Integer
intIllustrationsCount	20	Integer
conFiguresPerPage	2	Integer
conIllustrationsPerPage	4	Integer
intArtPages	5	Integer
intTotalPages	0	Integer

variables or expressions. To do so, you can use the Watch window, which lets
you set *watch expressions*, items which you want to monitor. Follow these steps:

1. In your macro, right-click the variable or expression you want to
    monitor, and then choose Add Watch from the context menu. The
    Visual Basic Editor displays the Add Watch dialog box (see Figure 13-5)
    and enters the variable or expression in the Expression text box.

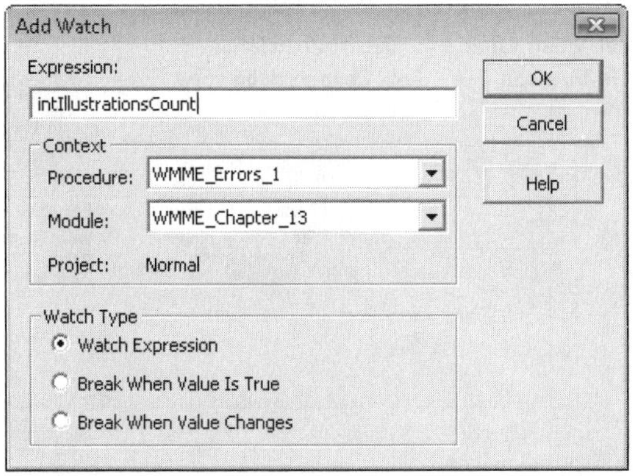

Add Watch

Expression:

intIllustrationsCount

Context

Procedure: WMME_Errors_1

Module: WMME_Chapter_13

Project: Normal

Watch Type

◉ Watch Expression

○ Break When Value Is True

○ Break When Value Changes

OK

Cancel

Help

Figure 13-5   The Add Watch
dialog box lets you set up
"watch expressions" you want
to monitor.

2. If you want to change the procedure for which you're monitoring the variable or expression, choose the procedure in the Procedure drop-down list. Similarly, if you want to change the module, choose the module in the Module drop-down list. Normally, you can just leave the default settings of the macro and procedure that contain the variable or expression.

3. In the Watch Type group box, choose the option button for the type of monitoring you want:

   ■ **Watch Expression**   Select this option button to add the variable or expression to the list in the Watch window.

   ■ **Break When Value Is True**   Select this option button to make VBA switch to Break mode when the variable's or expression's value becomes True. This setting is useful for expressions.

   ■ **Break When Value Changes**   Select this option button to make VBA switch to Break mode any time the value of the variable or expression changes at all.

4. Click the OK button to close the Add Watch window and add the watch expression to the Watch window, which the Visual Basic Editor displays automatically. Figure 13-6 shows the Watch window with several watch expressions.

**Break When Value   Break When Value
Is True icon   Changes icon**

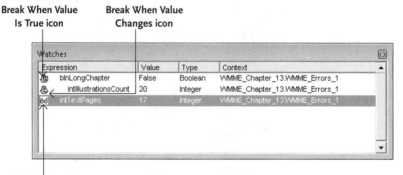

Figure 13-6   The Watch window lets you track particular variables and expressions as your macros run.

Watch Expression icon

5.   Run the macro, and see how the variables and expressions change. If you've set Break When Value Is True or Break When Value Changes watches, VBA enters Break mode if the condition is met.

6.   To remove a watch expression, right-click it in the Watch window and then choose Delete Watch. To edit a watch expression, right-click it in the Watch window and then choose Edit Watch to open it in the Edit Watch dialog box, which has the same controls as the Add Watch dialog box.

7.   When you've finished watching variables and expressions with the Watch window, click the window's Close button (the × button) to close it.

Use the Call Stack Dialog Box to See Which Macros and Functions You're Calling

When you write a macro that calls several other macros or functions, it becomes easy to lose track of all the different code items that are running. To help you keep track, the Visual Basic Editor provides the Call Stack dialog box.

Try this example of creating a macro that calls another macro that then calls a third macro:

```
Sub WMME_Calling_Another_Macro_1()
    Call WMME_Calling_Another_Macro_2
End Sub

Sub WMME_Calling_Another_Macro_2()
    Call WMME_Calling_Another_Macro_3
End Sub

Sub WMME_Calling_Another_Macro_3()
    MsgBox "Hi! How are you today?"
End Sub
```

Click in the WMME_Calling_Another_Macro_1 macro and press F8 to start stepping through the code. You'll see the execution highlight jump to the

WMME_Calling_Another_Macro_2 macro and then to the WMME_Calling_Another_Macro_3 macro.

All of this is happening not only with short macros but with ones in the same module. But when macros call code in other modules, tracing what's happening becomes much harder.

To see what has called what, open the Call Stack dialog box (see Figure 13-7) by clicking the Call Stack button on the Debug toolbar or clicking the Display Call Stack Dialog Box button in the Locals window. You can then click a macro and click the Show button to close the Call Stack dialog box and go to that macro, or simply click the Close button to close the Call Stack dialog box.

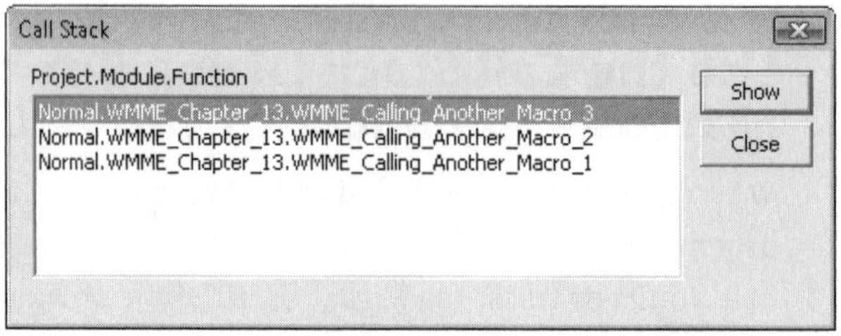

Figure 13-7 The Call Stack dialog box lets you trace calls from one macro to another.

Create an Error Handler

To take care of errors that occur when your macros run, you can create an *error handler*—a section of code that is specifically designed to catch errors and to deal with them. In this section, you'll create a simple error handler that catches an error and gives the user an easy way to deal with it.

Identify the Error You Want to Trap

Your first step is to identify the error you want to trap. In this example, we'll write a macro that tries to open a document that doesn't exist. Follow these steps:

1. Click in the Code window of your WMME_Chapter_13 module and type the stub of a macro named WMME_Using_an_Error_Handler:

```
Sub WMME_Using_an_Error_Handler()

End Sub
```

2. Inside the stub, declare a String variable named strFile, and then assign to it the folder path and filename of a document that doesn't exist. As usual, adapt the path to suit your file system.

```
Dim strFile As String
strFile =_
    "C:\Users\Ken\Documents\WMME\Error Document.docx"
```

3. Type a Documents.Open statement that tries to open the document identified by strFile:

```
Documents.Open FileName:= strFile, AddToRecentFiles:=False
```

4. Click in the macro and press F5 to run it. VBA displays a Microsoft Visual Basic dialog box giving you the error number (5174) and the error message ("This file could not be found."), as shown in Figure 13-8.

Microsoft Visual Basic

Run-time error '5174':

This file could not be found.
("C:\Users\Ken\...\Error Document.docx")

| Continue | End | Debug | Help |

Figure 13-8   You get this Microsoft Visual Basic dialog box when VBA can't find the document you ask to open.

5. Click the Debug button to close the Microsoft Visual Basic dialog box and go to the offending statement in the macro: the Documents.Open statement.

Set Up the Error Trap and Create the Handler

Your next move is to tell VBA that you want to trap errors. As you've just seen, until you tell VBA to trap errors, each error raises a dialog box.

To tell VBA you want to trap errors, you add an On Error statement before the statements that might produce errors. In our case, that means adding an On Error statement at the beginning of the macro, just after the variable declaration.

Follow these steps to trap the error and create the error handler:

1.   After the Dim strFile As String statement, add this On Error statement to trap the error:

     ```
     On Error GoTo MyErrorHandler
     ```

2.   After the Documents.Open statement, add the MyErrorHandler label (including the colon to indicate it's a label):

     ```
     MyErrorHandler:
     ```

3.   Create the following If statement that checks the Number property of the Err object (which contains the error) and, if the number is 5174, displays the Yes/No message box shown here, inviting the user to open another document manually. If the user clicks the Yes button, Word displays the Open dialog box so that the user can open a document. (Chapter 14 explains the details of using Word's built-in dialog boxes in this way.)

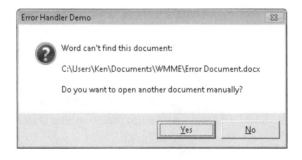

MEMO

If the error has a different number than 5174, the macro ends without displaying the message box or the Open dialog box.

```
    If Err.Number = 5174 Then
        If MsgBox("Word can't find this document:" & _
            vbCr & vbCr & strFile & vbCr & vbCr & _
            "Do you want to open another document manually?", _
            vbYesNo + vbQuestion, _
            "Error Handler Demo") = vbYes Then
            Dialogs(wdDialogFileOpen).Show
        End If
    End If
End If
```

The complete macro with the error handler looks like this:

```
Sub WMME_Using_an_Error_Handler()

    Dim strFile As String

    On Error GoTo MyErrorHandler

    strFile = _
        "C:\Users\Ken\Documents\WMME\Error Document.docx"
    Documents.Open FileName:=strFile, _
        AddToRecentFiles:=False

MyErrorHandler:
    If Err.Number = 5174 Then
        If MsgBox("Word can't find this document:" & _
            vbCr & vbCr & strFile & vbCr & vbCr & _
            "Do you want to open another document manually?", _
            vbYesNo + vbQuestion, _
            "Error Handler Demo") = vbYes Then
            Dialogs(wdDialogFileOpen).Show
        End If
    End If

End Sub
```

201

CARRY ON RUNNING CODE AFTER AN ERROR

Instead of using an On Error Goto statement and directing execution to an error handler, you can simply tell VBA to resume execution. You have three choices:

- **Resume Next** Normally the best choice, the Resume Next statement makes VBA resume execution at the line of code after the one that threw the error.

- **Resume** The Resume statement makes VBA resume execution at the same line. Normally,

you'll want to use a Resume statement only after running an error handler that fixes the problem—otherwise, the same error will simply occur again.

- **Resume** *line* The Resume *line* statement makes VBA resume execution at the *line*, which you specify with a label. For example, create a label named ResumeHere:, and then use Resume ResumeHere.

Step through the macro and watch what happens. Click the Yes button in the message box, and then use the Open dialog box to open a file. Step through the macro again, but this time click the No button in the message box, and watch the result.

Use Word's Built-In Dialog Boxes in Your Macros

In Chapter 4, you learned how to create dialog boxes containing the most useful controls, such as text boxes, check boxes, option buttons, and combo boxes.

Creating dialog boxes gives you great control, but there's no point in reinventing the wheel. When you need to perform standard Windows operations, you can simply borrow Word's own built-in dialog boxes and use them in your macros.

This way, everyone wins: you don't have to design, code, and debug a dialog box, and the users get to work with dialog boxes that they're familiar with. But you have a secret advantage: you can make the built-in dialog box behave in a *different* way than normal if you need to.

Get Set Up to Work Through This Chapter

In this chapter, you'll add built-in dialog boxes to the macro you recorded in the first chapter and edited in the third chapter. Here's what you'll do:

- Replace the part of the macro that opens a particular file with the Open dialog box so that the user can choose which file to open.

- Offer the user the option of printing the document they create. If they choose to print it, the macro will display the Print dialog box, in which they can choose print settings as usual.

- Let the user choose whether to save the document they've created or simply close it without saving changes.

To get set up so that you can work through this chapter, follow these steps:

1. Open Word and the Visual Basic Editor as usual. For example, launch Word from the Start menu, and then press ALT-F11 to open the Visual Basic Editor.

2. In the Project Explorer, expand the entry for the Normal template if it's collapsed.

3. Right-click the WMME_Chapter_3 module and then choose Export File from the context menu to display the Export File dialog box, as shown here with settings chosen.

4. Navigate to the WMME folder in your Documents folder (Windows Vista) or your My Documents folder (Windows XP).

5. Click the Save button. The Visual Basic Editor exports the module.

6. In the Project Explorer, right-click anywhere in the Normal template and then choose Import File from the context menu to display the Import File dialog box, as shown on the left here.

7. In the list box, click the WMME_Chapter_3 .bas file.

8. Click the Open button. The Visual Basic Editor imports the module into the Normal template. Because the name WMME_Chapter_3 is already in use, the Visual Basic Editor names the imported version WMME_Chapter_31.

9. In the Project Explorer, click the WMME_Chapter_31 module.

10. Press F4 to activate the Properties window and select the Name field.

11. Change the WMME_Chapter_31 name to WMME_Chapter_**14**, and then press ENTER to apply the change.

12. In the Code window, change the macro's name to **WMME_Transfer_ Data_with_Dialogs**.

Here's the code of the macro. Look back to Chapter 3 if you need to refresh your memory of what exactly the statements do. The folder path to the WMME folder will vary depending on whether you're using Windows Vista (the Documents folder) or Windows XP (the My Documents folder).

```
Sub WMME_Transfer_Data_with_Dialogs()
'
' WMME_Transfer_Data Macro
' Opens Latest Report.docx and copies data in it. Creates a new document,
pastes the copied data in it, and saves and closes the document.
'
```

```
        If MsgBox("Create a new report summary?", vbYesNo + vbQuestion, _
            "Transfer Data Macro") = vbYes Then
            Documents.Open _
                FileName:="C:\Users\Ken\Documents\WMME\Latest Report.docx", _
                ConfirmConversions:=False, ReadOnly:=False, _
                AddToRecentFiles:=False, PasswordDocument:="", _
                PasswordTemplate:="", Revert:=False, WritePasswordDocument:="", _
                WritePasswordTemplate:="", Format:=wdOpenFormatAuto, XMLTransform:=""
            Selection.MoveDown Unit:=wdParagraph, Count:=1
            Selection.MoveDown Unit:=wdParagraph, Count:=1, Extend:=wdExtend
            Selection.Copy
            ActiveDocument.Close
            Documents.Add DocumentType:=wdNewBlankDocument
            Selection.Style = ActiveDocument.Styles("Heading 1")
            Selection.TypeText Text:=InputBox("Type the title here:", _
                "Transfer Data Macro", "Report Summary")
            Selection.TypeParagraph
            Selection.TypeText Text:="Here is the latest report summary:"
            Selection.TypeParagraph
            Selection.PasteAndFormat (wdPasteDefault)
            ActiveDocument.SaveAs _
                FileName:="C:\Users\Ken\Documents\WMME\Report Summary.docx", _
                FileFormat:=wdFormatXMLDocument, LockComments:=False, Password:="", _
                AddToRecentFiles:=True, WritePassword:="", _
                ReadOnlyRecommended:=False, EmbedTrueTypeFonts:=False, _
                SaveNativePictureFormat:=False, SaveFormsData:=False, _
                SaveAsAOCELetter:=False
            ActiveDocument.Close
            MsgBox "The macro has created the report summary.", _
                vbOKOnly + vbInformation, "Transfer Data Macro"
        End If
    End Sub
```

Understand the Essentials of Using Word's Built-in Dialog Boxes

As you've seen throughout this book, VBA uses an object to represent each component of Word; and where there are multiple objects of the same kind, VBA groups them into a collection. So it will come as no surprise to learn that each Word dialog box is a Dialog object, and that you access the Dialog objects through the Dialogs collection.

Find the Name of the Dialog Box You Need

The dialog box name is derived from the days when Word had a full set of menus. For example, the Open dialog box is called wdDialogFileOpen (because you would choose File | Open to display the dialog box), and the Word Options dialog box is called wdDialogToolsOptions (Tools | Options). Because of the drastic changes the Ribbon makes to the Word user interface, you'll find the names easier to figure out if you have—or can remember—Word 2003 or an earlier version.

To help you with this, Table 14-1 gives you a short list of the dozen most useful dialog boxes out of the 200-odd that Word provides. (Your mileage will vary.)

Table 14-1   VBA Names for Word's 12 Most Useful Dialog Boxes

Dialog Box	VBA Name
New	wdDialogFileNew
Open	wdDialogFileOpen
Print	wdDialogFilePrint
Save As	wdDialogFileSaveAs
Find and Replace (Find tab)	wdDialogEditFind
Find and Replace (Replace tab)	wdDialogEditReplace
Find and Replace (Go To tab)	wdDialogEditGoTo
Paste Special	wdDialogEditPasteSpecial
Font	wdDialogFormatFont
Paragraph	wdDialogFormatParagraph
Insert Table	wdDialogTableInsertTable
Zoom	wdDialogViewZoom

HOW TO FIND THE OTHER BUILT-IN DIALOG BOXES

To find the names of all Word's built-in dialog boxes, search for the Built-in Dialog Box Argument Lists topic in VBA help. This topic shows the full list of dialog boxes and all the arguments you can use with them (more on these later in this chapter).

Not all of the dialog boxes on this list are available in Word 2007. For example, some are only in Mac versions of Word. Most of these have "Mac" in their names to indicate this, as in wdDialogFileMacPageSetup.

As when working in Word, you can display some dialog boxes (such as the Open dialog box) almost anytime via VBA. Other dialog boxes are available only when you've selected the appropriate object or when you're performing a particular process. For example, the various mail-merge dialog boxes are available only when you're working on mail-merge documents. If you try to display them at different times, VBA gives an error.

Understand the Different Ways of Displaying Built-in Dialog Boxes

Word lets you display dialog boxes in two different ways:

- Display the dialog box so that it runs just as it would normally. For example, you can display the Open dialog box so that the user can pick a document to open.

- Display the dialog box, retrieve the user's choices from it, and then implement the relevant choices. For example, you can display the Open dialog box, have the user select a document—but then delete the document rather than opening it. (This is just an example—I don't recommend doing this.)

Display a Dialog Box the Normal Way

To display a dialog box the normal way, you use the Show method. Try this example, in which you replace the VBA code for opening the Latest Report.docx document with the Open dialog box that lets the user open the document they want:

1. In the Code window for the WMME_Chapter_14 module, select the Documents.Open statement (all four lines of it), and then press DELETE to delete it.

2. In its place, type the following statement, using VBA's code-completion features to help enter the constant for the dialog box:

```
Dialogs(wdDialogFileOpen).Show
```

3. This will display the Open dialog box—but first, it would be useful to change the directory to your WMME folder, so that the right documents appear in the Open dialog box. Add a ChangeFileOpenDirectory statement before the Dialogs statement, copying the folder path from the ActiveDocument.SaveAs statement later in the macro. Here's an example:

```
ChangeFileOpenDirectory "C:\Users\Ken\Documents\WMME"
Dialogs(wdDialogFileOpen).Show
```

4. Press F5 or click the Run Sub/UserForm button to run the macro. After you click the Yes button in the initial message box, Word displays the Open dialog box, showing the contents of your WMME folder.

5. Select the Latest Report.docx document, and then click the Open button. Word opens the document, and the rest of the macro runs as normal.

DISPLAY A TAB OF A BUILT-IN DIALOG BOX

When you display a built-in dialog box that contains tabs, you can use the DefaultTab property to control which tab appears at the front of the dialog box.

The tab name is the dialog box's name, followed by "tab" and then by either the literal name of the tab or a descriptive name. For example, the Indents And Spacing tab of the Paragraph dialog box is called wdDialogFormatParagraphTabIndentsAndSpacing, but the Line And Page Breaks tab is called wdDialogFormatParagraphTabTextFlow. (Microsoft has changed tab names over the years but kept the VBA names the same so that code works as consistently as possible.) The easiest way to find the tab names is by using Word's code-completion features.

For example, click in the Code window below your WMME_Transfer_Data_with_Dialogs macro and type the following macro, which displays the Line And Page Breaks tab of the Paragraph dialog box:

```
Sub WMME_Dialog_Tab()
    With Dialogs(wdDialogFormatParagraph)
        .DefaultTab = wdDialog
FormatParagraphTabIndentsAndSpacing
        .Show
        .DefaultTab =
wdDialogFormatParagraphTabTextFlow
        .Show
    End With
End Sub
```

Make sure you have a document open in Word. Then click in the macro and press F5 or click the Run Sub/UserForm button to run it.

The first Show statement displays the Indents and Spacing tab of the Paragraph dialog box. Click the Cancel button to close the dialog box. The second Show statement displays the Line and Page Breaks tab of the Paragraph dialog box. Click the Cancel button again.

Display a Dialog Box and Retrieve Its Settings

The second way to display a dialog box is to make the dialog box appear so that the user can make choices in it, but not have the dialog box perform the actions unless you choose to perform them. Instead, you retrieve the user's choices from the dialog box and take whichever actions you need to.

MEMO

Users may find this behavior confusing, so it's a good idea to warn them first. For example, display a message box telling the user that the Open dialog box will appear so that they can select a document—but that the macro will then process the document rather than opening it.

To display a dialog box without executing the user's choices, you use the Display method of the appropriate Dialog object. After the user clicks the button to dismiss the dialog box, you can check the settings that the user chose and take action accordingly. If the settings are suitable for whatever you're doing, you can use the Execute method to "execute" the dialog box—in other words, implement the settings.

As it stands, the example macro saves the document it has created under the name Latest Report.docx. Follow these steps to make the macro display the Save As dialog box so that the user can choose the filename:

1. In the ActiveDocument.SaveAs statement, select the folder path and filename after the FileName argument (including the double quotation marks) and press CTRL-C to copy it to the Clipboard.

2. Select the ActiveDocument.SaveAs statement (all five lines of it), and then press DELETE to delete it.

3. Press ENTER to create a new line where the statement was, and then type this With statement on that line:

```
With Dialogs(wdDialogFileSaveAs)
    .Display
End With
```

Click in the macro, and then press F5 or click the Run Sub/UserForm button to run it. At the end of the macro, the Save As dialog box appears, apparently as normal, so that you can choose a folder and filename for the new document. But you'll notice that when you click the Save button and close the dialog box, the document doesn't get saved—and then when the ActiveDocument.Close statement goes to close the macro, it prompts you to decide whether to save changes. Click the No button so that VBA can finish running the macro.

Choose and Check Settings in a Built-in Dialog Box

Before displaying a built-in dialog box, you may want to set some of the settings it contains—for example, to encourage the user to use the macro as you intend.

Find Out What the Settings Are Called

To change a setting, you specify the value for the appropriate argument. To find the arguments, follow these steps:

1. Click in the Help box in the upper-right corner of the Visual Basic Editor window.

2. Type **dialog box argument list** and press ENTER.

3. In the Word Help window, click the Built-in Dialog Box Argument Lists topic.

4. Scroll down to the dialog box you want, and find the argument you need.

Choose Settings in a Built-in Dialog Box

Try this example of choosing two settings in the Save As dialog box you added to the macro:

1. Click in the With Dialogs(wdDialogFileSaveAs) statement before the .Display statement, and press ENTER to create a new line.

2. On the new line, type a ChangeFileOpenDirectory statement and paste in the path you copied to the Clipboard, deleting the filename. For example:

```
ChangeFileOpenDirectory "C:\Users\Ken\Documents\WMME\"
```

3. On the next line, type **.format = 0**, so that you have this:

```
With Dialogs(wdDialogFileSaveAs)
    ChangeFileOpenDirectory "C:\Users\Ken\Documents\WMME\"
    .Format = 0
    .Display
End With
```

4. Press F5 to test the macro. This time, when the Save As dialog box appears, the Save As Type drop-down list has the Word 97–2003 Document (*.doc) format selected.

5. Change the statement to **.Format = 12** and run the macro again. This time, the Save As Type drop-down list has the Word Document (*.docx) format selected, which is probably the best choice.

Check the Settings the User Chose

After the user has clicked a button to close the dialog box, you can check the settings they've chosen. You can do this for either the Show method or the Display method, but it's usually much more use for the Display method, because you can then take actions accordingly; with the Show method, the horse will typically already have bolted.

For example, when the user closes the Save As dialog box, you may want to check that the user hasn't chosen the wrong file format. Try changing your With Dialogs(wdDialogFileSaveAs) statement so that it looks like this (apart from the folder path):

```
With Dialogs(wdDialogFileSaveAs)
    ChangeFileOpenDirectory "C:\Users\Ken\Documents\WMME\"
    .Format = 12
    .Display
    If .Format <> 12 Then
        If .Format <> 0 Then
            .Format = 12
        End If
    End If
End With
```

After the .Display statement displays the Save As dialog box, the If statement checks to see if the format is not 12 (the Word .docx format). If it's not, the nested If statement checks to see if the format is not 0 (the Word 97–2003 document format), which is okay too. If the format isn't 0 either, the macro changes the format to 12, so that the document will be saved in Word .docx format.

To execute the dialog box's settings, you can add an .Execute statement, like this:

```
.Execute
```

But first, you'll probably want to check that the user didn't click the Cancel button in the Save As dialog box, as described next.

Find Out Which Button the User Clicked in a Built-in Dialog Box

To find out which button the user clicked in a dialog box, check the return value VBA assigns to the Display method or the Show method. Table 14-2 shows the values.

Table 14-2   Return Values from Built-in Dialog Boxes

Button Clicked	Return Value
OK	−1
Cancel	0
Close	−2
First command button (other than OK, Cancel, or Close)	1
Second command button (other than OK, Cancel, or Close)	2

For example, the Save As dialog box has a Save button and a Cancel button. Clicking the Save button or pressing ENTER returns −1, and clicking the Cancel button or pressing ESC returns 0.

Change the end of your macro so that it looks like this (apart from the folder path):

```
With Dialogs(wdDialogFileSaveAs)
    ChangeFileOpenDirectory "C:\Users\Ken\Documents\WMME\"
    .Format = 12
    If .Display = -1 Then
        If .Format <> 12 Then
            If .Format <> 0 Then
                .Format = 12
            End If
        End If
        .Execute
        ActiveDocument.Close
        MsgBox "The macro has created the report summary.", _
            vbOKOnly + vbInformation, "Transfer Data Macro"
    End If
End With
```

By now, you can quickly grasp what happens:

- The ChangeFileOpenDirectory statement sets the folder in which the macro encourages the user to save the document. (Again, you'll have your own folder here.)

- The .Format = 12 statement makes the Save As Type drop-down list show Word Document (*.docx) at first.

- The If Display = –1 Then statement displays the Save As dialog box and checks its return value to see if the user clicked the Save button or pressed ENTER. If this is the case, the rest of the code runs, checking the format, executing the settings in the dialog box, closing the document, and displaying the message box. If not, the user must have clicked the Cancel button or pressed ESC, in which case the macro simply leaves the document open and unsaved.

SET A TIMEOUT FOR A BUILT-IN DIALOG BOX

Sometimes you may want to make a built-in dialog box appear for a short length of time, then close it automatically if the user is not present to close it manually. You can do this by using the TimeOut argument and specifying the time in milliseconds.

Click in the Code window below your WMME_ Transfer_Data_with_Dialogs macro and type the following macro:

```
Sub WMME_Dialog_Timeout()
    Dialogs(wdDialogFilePrint).Show
TimeOut:=5000
End Sub
```

Click in the macro and press F5 or click the Run Sub/UserForm button to run the macro. You'll see Word open the Print dialog. Wait five seconds, and Word closes it again.

The TimeOut argument works only for some built-in dialog boxes, so test it to make sure it works with the dialog box you've chosen.

Right-click the If .Format <> 12 Then statement and then choose Toggle | Breakpoint from the context menu to set a breakpoint. (If you don't do this, VBA executes the whole of the If .Display statement at once when you close the Save As dialog box even if you're stepping through the macro.) Then press F8 to step through the macro twice. Test what happens both when you click the Save button and when you click the Cancel button.

Share Your Macros with Others

Once you've created powerful macros that save you time and effort, you'll probably want to share them with your colleagues so that they can save time and effort too. This chapter shows you how to share your macros.

In an ideal world, sharing your macros would be easy. But because macro viruses can do huge amounts of damage, Microsoft has built into the Office programs security mechanisms that make sharing harder.

So before you can share your macros effectively, you need to understand Word's security features. You may need to change the security settings on your PC so that you can work with macros; likewise, you may need to adjust the Office security settings on your colleagues' PCs (or have your colleagues adjust them) before they can run the macros you've developed.

To get the macros onto your colleagues' computers, you may need to move macros from one document or template to another. You will probably also have to sign your macros with digital signatures to prove that you created them.

MEMO

VBA is by no means the only macro language that can be exploited by virus writers, but because Office and VBA are so widely used, they're the most popular targets for malefactors. In particular, because Outlook can be controlled via VBA, it's one of the easiest ways for a malefactor to spread a virus: Outlook (or one of the other VBA-enabled applications) can be programmed to automatically send messages to every entry in its address book. This can generate enough e-mail to crash even powerful corporate mail servers in short order.

Understand Why Macro Viruses Pose a Threat to Windows

As you've seen throughout this book, VBA and the Macro Recorder greatly increase Word's power, flexibility, and usefulness. Unfortunately, VBA and macros also expose Word (and other VBA-enabled applications) to the attentions of malefactors who create *macro viruses*—harmful code built using a macro language.

Macro viruses can be contained in frequently exchanged files—such as Word documents, Excel documents, or PowerPoint presentations—and can be triggered when the file is opened, closed, or otherwise manipulated. So whenever anyone sends you a file, you should check it for macro viruses using an antivirus program.

Macro viruses can spread themselves in several ways. Some automatically add themselves surreptitiously to your existing documents and insert themselves into new documents you create. When you share a document with another user, that user's computer becomes infected with the virus as well and can spread it further. Other macro viruses take a more aggressive approach, using a programmable e-mail application such as Outlook to send themselves to as many people as possible as an apparently normal or attractive document attached to a suitable e-mail message. For example, a macro virus designed to spread in a corporate environment might disguise itself as a routine document such as a memo or spreadsheet. A macro designed to spread anywhere might appeal to recipients' curiosity by pretending to contain—or actually containing—jokes or smut.

To protect its users against macro viruses, Office includes antivirus features. To use macros and VBA, you need to understand what these features are and how they work.

Understand and Set Security Levels

Office uses a four-part security mechanism for preventing harmful code from being run by an Office application:

MEMO

Office's antivirus features provide *some* protection against macros written in VBA, but there are plenty of non-VBA types of viruses, scripts, and other *malware* (malicious software) that can damage your software or hardware. So even with Office's antivirus measures turned on, you should use third-party antivirus software to protect your computer.

■ **Security level**   You can set security levels to specify whether an installation of Office may or may not run code that might be harmful. You can set a different security level in each Office application, if you wish. For example, you might set Word to use the Medium security level but set Excel to use the High security level.

■ **Digital signature**   You can sign a VBA project (a unit of VBA code) with a digital signature derived from a digital certificate to prove that you were the last person who changed that VBA project. This digital signature tells other people the source of the VBA project. If other people have reason to trust you, they may trust the code you've signed.

■ **Trusted locations**   You can tell a particular Office program (for example, Word) that certain folders are *trusted locations*—folders that you guarantee will never contain unsafe code. Word then allows you to run code in documents contained in those trusted locations.

■ **Trusted publishers**   You can designate certain digital certificates as being *trusted publishers*, telling the Office security mechanism to trust any code signed with one of those digital certificates. Again, you're telling the Office application that you're taking responsibility for the safeness of the code.

As you can see, these security measures are intertwined. The following sections discuss how you work with them.

Set the Security Level for Running VBA Code

To set the security level that Word uses for macros, follow these steps:

1. Click the Microsoft Office button and then click Word Options. Word displays the Word Options dialog box.

2. In the left panel, click the Trust Center category, and then click the Trust Center Settings button. Word displays the Macro Settings category in the Trust Center dialog box, shown next.

219

3. In the Macro Settings area, select an option button to tell Word how to handle macros contained in documents stored in folders that are not trusted locations. Take the following into consideration when you make your choice:

■ Usually, the best choice for someone who uses macros is the Disable All Macros With Notification option button, which disables all macros and displays a Security Warning bar to let you know that it has done so. (The sidebar "Enable Blocked Macros" shows an example of the Security Warning bar.) You can choose to enable the macros or leave them disabled.

■ The Disable All Macros Without Notification option button makes Word disable the macros but give you no indication that it has done so. This setting is useful for users who should not receive documents containing macros and, even if they do, should certainly not run such macros.

■ In a corporate environment, an administrator may set up Word using the Disable All Macros Except Digitally Signed Macros option button to ensure that you can run only macros that have been tested, approved, and signed.

■ The Enable All Macros option button is a setting that only security researchers working on cordoned-off computers should use.

4. In the Developer Macro Settings area, clear the Trust Access To The VBA Project Object Model check box unless you're creating your own macros in the Visual Basic Editor (as opposed to using the Macro Recorder, as described in this chapter).

5. Leave the Trust Center dialog box open so that you can verify your trusted locations, as described in the next section.

ENABLE BLOCKED MACROS

If you choose the Disable All Macros With Notification option button in the Macro Settings category in the Trust Center dialog box, Word displays a Security Warning bar below the Ribbon when it disables macros. Here's an example:

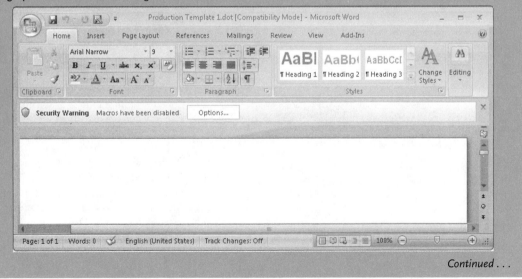

Continued . . .

If you don't need to use the macros (or if you don't know what they are), you can leave them blocked by simply clicking the Close button (the × button) on the Security Warning bar. But if you want to enable the macros, click the Options button. Word displays the Microsoft Office Security Options: Security Alert – Macro dialog box. If the document is signed with a digital signature, but the digital signature is invalid, the dialog box looks like this, with only the Help Protect Me From Unknown Content option button available:

If the digital signature is valid, but it's from a publisher that you haven't yet specified you trust, the Security Alert – Macro dialog box looks like the next dialog box.

If the document doesn't have a digital signature, the Security Alert – Macro dialog box contains the Help Protect Me From Unknown Content option button and the Enable This Content option button, but not the Signature box or the Trust All Documents From This Publisher option button.

If the Signature box appears (as in the example here), examine the details of the digital certificate, and then decide whether this is a person or company you can trust. To see the details of the digital certificate, click the Show Signature Details link. Word displays the Digital Signature Details dialog box.

For either a signed document with a valid signature or an unsigned document, select the Enable This Content option button if you want to enable the content for this document. If the document has a digital signature, you can also select the Trust All Documents From This Publisher option button to tell Word to add the holder of this digital certificate to your list of trusted publishers.

Click the OK button. If you chose to enable the macros, Word enables them.

NOTE

In a corporate environment, an administrator may prevent you from adding or changing trusted locations and trusted publishers.

Verify Your List of Trusted Locations

To enable yourself to run the macros you need to run, verify the folders that Word is set to regard as trusted locations. You may need to add other folders to the list, or even remove existing folders that you no longer want to trust.

To verify your trusted locations, follow these steps:

1. In the Trust Center dialog box, click the Trusted Locations category in the left panel. Word displays the Trusted Locations list (see Figure 15-1).

Trust Center

Trusted Publishers	**Trusted Locations**		
Trusted Locations	Warning: All these locations are treated as trusted sources for opening files. If you change or add a location, make sure that the new location is secure.		
Add-ins			
ActiveX Settings	Path	Description	Date Modified
Macro Settings	**User Locations**		
Message Bar	C:\...\Ken\AppData\Roaming\Microsoft\Templates\	Word 2007 default location: User Templates	
Privacy Options	C:\Program Files\Microsoft Office\Templates\	Word 2007 default location: Application Templates	
	C:\...n\AppData\Roaming\Microsoft\Word\Startup\	Word 2007 default location: StartUp	

Policy Locations

Path: C:\Users\Ken\AppData\Roaming\Microsoft\Templates\
Description: Word 2007 default location: User Templates

Date Modified:
Sub Folders: Disallowed

[Add new location...] [Remove] [Modify...]

☐ Allow Trusted Locations on my network (not recommended)
☐ Disable all Trusted Locations. Only files signed by Trusted Publishers will be trusted.

[OK] [Cancel]

223

Figure 15-1 The Trusted Locations category in the Trust Center dialog box lets you tell Word which folders contain trustworthy code.

2. Look through the folders to make sure that you want to trust all of them. If the Path readout in the list doesn't show the full path to the folder, click the entry to select it, and then look at the Path readout below the list box. Word normally trusts the following folders, but an administrator may have added further trusted locations to this list:

- **User Templates folder** This folder contains your user templates—the templates you create or download. In a corporate environment, an administrator may have removed this folder from the list of trusted locations.

■ **Startup folder** This folder contains your personal items to be loaded when Word starts—for example, any global templates that you require other than the Normal template. In a corporate environment, an administrator may have removed this folder from the list of trusted locations.

■ **Application Templates folder** This folder contains the templates installed automatically by Office.

■ **Policy Locations list** This list shows folders that have been added via group policy, a tool that Windows network administrators use to configure Windows and applications across a network. (If your PC doesn't connect to a Windows Server–based network, this item doesn't appear.)

3. To add a trusted location to the list, follow these steps:

■ Click the Add New Location button. Word displays the Microsoft Office Trusted Location dialog box, shown here with choices made:

■ In the Path text box, enter the path to the folder. If you wish, you can type the path, but it's usually easier to click the Browse button, use the Browse dialog box to select the folder, and then click the OK button.

- If you want Word to trust the contents of any subfolders this folder contains, select the Subfolders Of This Location Are Also Trusted check box. If you keep documents that contain macros in a hierarchy of folders, you need to either select this check box for the parent (topmost) folder or designate each folder in the hierarchy as a trusted location.

- In the Description text box, type a description of the trusted location. This description appears in the Trusted Locations list to help you identify the trusted location.

- Click the OK button. Word closes the Microsoft Office Trusted Location dialog box and adds the trusted location to the Trusted Locations list.

4. To remove a trusted location, select it in the Trusted Locations list and then click the Remove button.

5. To modify a trusted location, select it in the Trusted Locations list and then click the Modify button. Word displays the Microsoft Office Trusted Location box, in which you can change the folder or its description. The change you'll most often want to make is to select the Subfolders Of This Location Are Also Trusted check box for the folder. For example, you might need to trust the subfolders of your User Templates folder, because Word does not trust these subfolders by default.

6. If you need to work with documents or templates containing code that are stored in folders on your network, select the Allow Trusted Locations On My Network check box. Unless you control your entire network (for example, it's your home network), this setting may expose your computer to code that others create. If you can keep all your code in folders on your hard drive, leave this check box cleared.

225

7. Clear the Disable All Trusted Locations, Only Files Signed By Trusted Publishers Will Be Trusted check box if you need to work with your own code. Selecting this check box gives Word tight security, but it makes developing your own macros hard work.

8. Leave the Trust Center dialog box open so that you can verify your trusted publishers, as described in the next section.

Designate Trusted Publishers for VBA Code

The Trusted Publishers category in the Trust Center dialog box (see Figure 15-2) lists the publishers you or your administrator have specified as being trusted. In this context, a *publisher* means the holder of a particular digital certificate. Click the View button to display the details of a selected publisher, or click the Remove button to remove a selected publisher you no longer want to trust.

Figure 15-2   Use the Trusted Publishers category in the Trust Center dialog box to examine, manage, and remove trusted publishers.

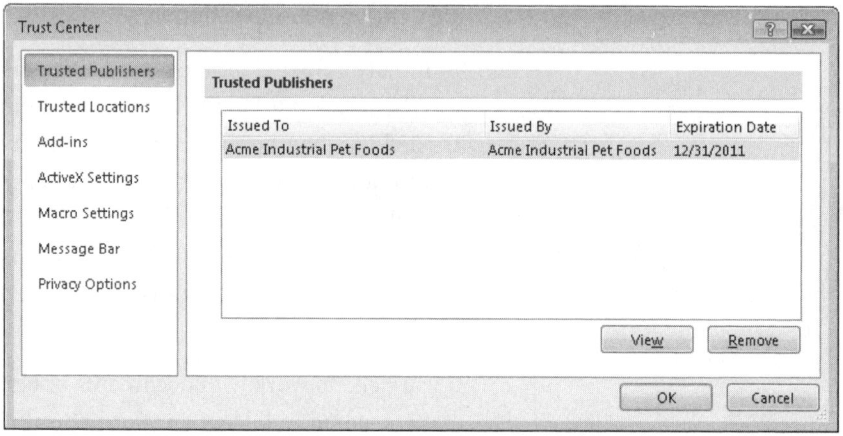

MEMO

The list of trusted publishers is applied across all Windows applications and features that use digital certificates. So if you add a trusted publisher in Word, Excel and PowerPoint trust that publisher too.

You can add trusted publishers to your Windows installation by selecting the Trust All Documents From This Publisher option button in the Microsoft Office Security Options: Security Alert – Macro dialog box, as discussed earlier in this chapter.

Move a Macro to a Different Document or Template

Before distributing a macro, you'll often need to move it to a different document or template. Word provides two ways of doing so:

■ **Move the macro manually**   Open the macro in the Visual Basic Editor, as you've been doing throughout this book. Select the macro's code, copy or cut it, and then paste it into a module in the other document or template.

■ **Use the Organizer to move the module that contains the macro**   The process is simple, but you have to move an entire module: You cannot move just a macro.

To move a module and all the macros it contains, follow these steps:

1. Open the document or template that contains the module. If the module is in a template, open either the template itself or (easier) a document to which the template is attached.

2. Open the document or template to which you want to move the module. If the destination is a template, you need only open a document to which the template is attached.

3. Choose Developer | Code | Macros or press ALT-F8. Word displays the Macros dialog box.

4. Click the Organizer button. Word displays the Organizer dialog box (see Figure 15-3) with the Macro Project Items tab foremost.

5. In the Macro Project Items Available In drop-down list on either the left side or the right side of the Organizer dialog box, select the document or template that contains the module. The In list box on that side shows the modules and other code items the document or template contains.

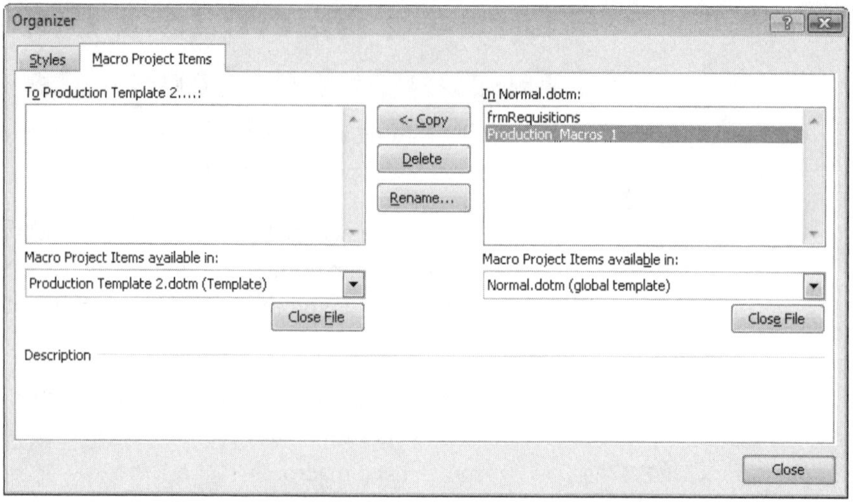

Figure 15-3 The Macro Project Items tab of the Organizer dialog box lets you move a code module from one document or template to another. You can also rename or delete a code module. But you cannot move a macro on its own.

THE EASY WAY

You can open another document or template by clicking either the left or right Close File button, clicking the Open File button that replaces it, and then selecting the document or template. But usually it's much easier to open both documents or templates before displaying the Organizer dialog box.

6. In the other Macro Project Items Available In drop-down list, select the destination document or template. The To list box on that side shows the modules and other code items the document or template contains.

7. In the first list box, select the module you want to move, copy, delete, or rename.

8. Click the appropriate button:

   ■ To move or copy the module, click the Copy button. To move the module, copy the module like that, then click the Delete button to delete the module from the source document or template, and confirm the deletion.

   ■ To delete the module, click the Delete button, and then confirm the deletion.

   ■ To rename the module, click the Rename button, type the new name in the Rename dialog box, and then click the OK button.

9. When you've finished working with the Organizer dialog box, click the Close button.

10. SHIFT-click the Microsoft Office button, and then choose Save All from the menu to save all the changes you've made to the documents and templates.

Understand and Use Digital Signatures

As you saw earlier in this chapter, the Office security mechanism uses a digital signature on a macro project to determine whether the source of the project is trusted (and, therefore, whether you can use the project or not). In this section, you'll learn what a digital signature is and how you get a digital certificate for applying a digital signature.

Understand What Digital Certificates Are and What They're For

A digital signature is derived from a *digital certificate*, an encrypted piece of code intended to identify its holder. That holder may be an individual, a group of individuals, a department, or an entire company. Different types of digital certificates are available, including the following:

- **Personal certificates**   For signing and encrypting e-mail messages
- **Software developer certificates**   For signing macros and software
- **Corporate certificates**   For identifying companies or parts of them

Digital certificates aren't foolproof, but they provide reasonably effective security. Digital certificates are issued by *certification authorities* (CAs) and are only as reliable as the CAs choose to make them. For example, some CAs let you buy a personal digital certificate over the Web without providing any more verification than a credit card number and its current expiry date.

This standard of verification is satisfactory for telephone and Internet mail order because the physical address to which the goods are delivered corroborates the information on the credit card (assuming the goods are delivered to the card's billing address). But for proving identity via the Internet, this standard of verification is woefully unsatisfactory.

Software developer certificates and corporate certificates typically require better proof of identity than this, but again they usually leverage existing means of identification (for example, passports or other identity cards for individuals, business listings such as Dun & Bradstreet for companies, and so on) rather than checking rigorously from scratch. Another problem is that a digital certificate can be stolen from its holder, used by someone else without the holder's permission, applied inadvertently by its holder, or applied by *malware* (hostile software) running on the holder's computer.

Get and Install a Digital Certificate

The five main public sources of digital certificates at the time of this writing are

- **VeriSign** (www.verisign.com)
- **Thawte** (www.thawte.com; a VeriSign company)
- **GeoTrust** (www.geotrust.com; a VeriSign company)
- **Comodo** (www.comodo.com)
- **GoDaddy** (www.godaddy.com)

If your company requires that you use a digital certificate in your work, it may well run a CA of its own. For example, Windows Server provides CA features.

When you acquire a digital certificate, you'll need to install it on your computer before you can use it. The certificate-issuing routines that some CAs use automatically install the certificate for you. To install the certificate manually, double-click the certificate's file and follow the steps in the Certificate Import Wizard, which Windows launches.

CREATE YOUR OWN DIGITAL CERTIFICATE FOR OFFICE

Office includes a tool called Digital Certificate for VBA Projects that enables you to create your own digital certificates to practice signing code. This is a useful practice tool, but the certificate is useless in the real world, because your identity isn't authenticated. As a result, Office trusts a certificate created with Digital Certificate for VBA Projects only on the computer that created the certificate.

Digital Certificate for VBA Projects is included in Complete installations of Office. For other installations, you may need to install it by rerunning the Office installation program. Expand the Office Shared Features category, click the drop-down button on the Digital Signature For VBA Projects item, and then choose Run From My Computer from the menu.

Once Digital Certificate for VBA Projects is installed, you can run it by choosing Start | All Programs | Microsoft Office | Microsoft Office Tools | Digital Certificate For VBA Projects. In the Create Digital Certificate dialog box (shown here), type the name you want to assign to the certificate, and then click the OK button.

Digital Certificate for VBA Projects displays a SelfCert Success dialog box (the application's filename is SelfCert.exe) telling you that the certificate was created. The application also installs the certificate automatically for you, so you don't need to install it manually.

231

Sign a Word Document or Template with a Digital Signature

Before distributing your macros to your colleagues, it's a good idea to sign the project that contains them with a digital signature issued by or approved by your company. By signing the project, you can make Word treat your macros as trusted rather than as suspicious, and your colleagues can keep Word's defenses in place rather than trust untrustworthy code.

To sign a document or template with a digital signature, follow these steps:

1.   Open the document or template and make it active.

2.   Press ALT-F11. Word opens the Visual Basic Editor and selects the project for the active document or template in the Project Explorer window in the upper-left corner of the Visual Basic Editor window.

3. Choose Tools | Digital Signature. The Visual Basic Editor displays the Digital Signature dialog box.

4. Click the Choose button. The Visual Basic Editor displays the Select Certificate dialog box:

5. Click the certificate you want (click the View Certificate button if you want to see more of the certificate's details), and then click the OK button. The Visual Basic Editor closes the Select Certificate dialog box and returns you to the Digital Signature dialog box, which now shows the certificate you chose.

6. Click the OK button. The Visual Basic Editor closes the Digital Signature dialog box.

7. Choose File | Close And Return To Microsoft Word. The Visual Basic Editor closes, and the Word window becomes active.

8. Press CTRL-S or click the Save button on the Quick Access Toolbar to save the change to the project.

MEMO

If you change the code in a project, you will need to apply the digital signature again. The digital signature certifies that the code has not been changed since you applied the signature.

Index

References to figures are in italics.

235